K.I.C.K.
Your Fear
of Horses

By
Heidi A. McLaughlin

Foreword written by
Chris Cox

ISBN: 1477598677

ISBN-13: 9781477598672

Disclaimer

While the techniques and methods described in this book are drawn from the author's extensive experience and research, this book is not all-inclusive on the subject matter and may not apply in all circumstances. This book is not intended to be a training manual. The reader should consult with and seek the advice of a professional trainer or competent horseperson when considering applying these techniques on his or her particular horse or in a specific circumstance. Neither the author nor the publisher assume any liability or make any guarantees of any nature for outcome resulting from the use of the procedures or techniques described herein.

Dedication

To my best friend and husband, Pete, who has stood by me for over 35 years and who continually encourages me to pursue my passions and follow my dreams. Who believes in me even when I don't believe in myself. Who protects and cares for me and believes that his sole purpose in life is to make me happy! I love you.

Acknowledgments

In the course of writing this book, I found that there were many more people than I had originally thought, who were plagued with horse fear. I want to thank those of you who were willing to allow me to profile your stories and follow your progress. I am also very grateful for the willingness of some of the world's greatest horsemen and horsewomen, who eagerly agreed to give their expert advice to me to print in this book in the hopes of helping people with horse fear, gain the confidence they need to ride with joy. And I want to thank those of you who went way beyond the call of duty to help me with this project. I will never forget the way you gave of your time, talent and treasure. Without you, this would not have been possible!

Table of Contents

Foreword . . . . *xi*

Introduction . . . . *xiii*

Chapter 1   *Define Your Fear and Admit It!* *1*

Chapter 2   *It's Not the Horse!* *11*

Chapter 3   *K.I.C.K.* *19*

Chapter 4   *Continue to Learn and Grow!* *35*

Chapter 5   *Learning About Yourself!* *43*

Chapter 6   *Green on Green* *51*

Chapter 7   *From Fear Into Confidence!* *59*

Chapter 8   *The Women Speak!* *73*

Chapter 9   *Let's Hear It From the Boys!* *85*

Chapter 10 *Practical Secrets to Success* *93*

Author's Note *113*

In Memory of "The Cadillac" *119*

Chris Cox and author, Heidi A. McLaughlin

Foreword

Ifirst met Heidi McLaughlin in 2002 when she attended the first of several of my week-long horsemanship clinics. She was eager to learn but her fear kept getting in the way of her progress. I pushed her over and over to rise up and face her fear. The result was the beginning of her journey into the confidence that I want for all riders.

K.I.C.K. Your Fear of Horses is heart-warming and honest as well as entertaining. Heidi speaks frankly about the depth of her fear and walks the reader through her journey that started out being plagued with frustration and self-doubt. As a result, she understands fear from the depth of her being and therefore is able to give practical advice of what worked for her as well as important information that helped transform her into the successful rider that she is today.

I am proud of Heidi's success. Her talent for writing and her passion for horses give her an edge that is a perfect combination for this must-read! My hope is that all who read *K.I.C.K. Your Fear of Horses* can find the confidence and joy that she has found with her horses.

- Chris Cox

Author of the bestseller **Ride The Journey**, three-time winner of **Road to the Horse** Championship title, and whose motto **"Building Confidence Through Knowledge"** has helped thousands of people around the country with his proven natural horsemanship methods.

Introduction

From as far back as I can remember I have been crazy about horses! I was born with a deep passion for them that pierced my soul beyond anything I have ever been able to explain in words. The very sight of them always ignited a stirring, a longing, and a need to be near them. It is a feeling that I have never been able to deny.

When I was a child I had a collection of Breyer plastic horses that adorned my window sill. Every birthday and every Christmas I asked for another "horse" to add to my collection. My over-preoccupation with horses caused concern to my mother who nearly took me to a psychologist because I thought I *was* a horse. I whinnied, pawed the ground, and galloped around all day long. But since my mother was a ballet teacher, *my* ballet teacher, horseback riding lessons were out of the question. Instead I spent my entire childhood immersed in intensive professional ballet training whether I liked it or not.

My grandparents, bless their souls, had a small ranch in Lucerne Valley in the Mojave desert of Southern California where they kept a pony for me and my cousins along with a couple of barn sour ranch horses. Any exposure that I had to feed my horse-loving soul was through my grandparents who, I now realize, were not experts in the field!

My very first solo horseback riding experience was when I was about 8 years old. It was a beautiful sunny day as I started out on a trail ride on a jet-black 17-hand Tennessee Walker named Lopez. I remember feeling somewhat nervous but my grandfather was riding next to me on his Quarter Horse. Things seemed to be going along pretty well until we rounded the final corner of the trail and pointed towards home. At first, when Lopez began to trot I felt an instant surge of panic because I had no instinctive idea of what I was supposed to do nor did I have any practical knowledge of what to do either. Yes, I had been told you kick a horse to go and pull back on the reins and say "whoa" to stop. How hard could it be?

So when the horse felt no direction or control from me he naturally increased his gait. I remember frantically grabbing the saddle horn for dear life as Lopez exploded into a full gallop. I began screaming and continued to scream in sheer terror as this out-of-control, huge and powerful animal continued thundering down the trail. My thoughts were a blur and the more I screamed the more frightened poor Lopez became which made him run faster and faster simply to get us home and get me off of his back!

I had long since dropped the reins which had become tangled around Lopez's legs in all the commotion. And for some reason, that still remains a mystery to me, I thought in order to save myself, I simply needed to get off. Fast! So while the horse was in a full gallop I began trying to unseat myself to prepare to jump. Still holding onto the saddle horn I managed to slide my right leg from the right stirrup and ended up with two feet in the left stirrup. (It was because of this stunt that I earned the nick-name "trick rider"!) I ended up with bruises on my cheek bone from the saddle horn banging against my face in keeping with the rhythm of the horse's powerful gait. I was just about to jump off when Lopez finally arrived at the barn and came to a screeching halt in front of the gate. My grandmother came running towards us screaming who-knows-what and frantically waving her arms.

She grabbed hold of Lopez's bridle and told me to hurry and run off as if the horse was about to eat me! As I tried to run to safety my knees gave out and I fell down to the ground. I shook uncontrollably for what seemed like hours afterwards as the blood slowly returned to my face. I couldn't understand what had happened; what went wrong? Needless to say, the whole ordeal scared the living heck out of me and so planted the seed that instilled my deep fear of horses that would take nearly 40 years to undo.

That fateful day on Lopez before he ran away with me.

Just about everything that could have gone wrong did on that day. Not a good first horse experience for anyone. Thus pointing out the obvious; there is an inherent risk when riding horses, they are large and powerful animals, and you must know what you are doing if you are going to ride them. Obviously there is more to it than kick to go and pull back to stop. None of this is a secret. Right?

Do you want to know what the secret to fearless riding is? In a word: Knowledge. Knowledge is power! And fear is no more than that which is unknown to us.

Let's break down my Lopez story and look at it for what it was: A recipe for disaster!

1. **The first time in the saddle by myself, I should not have been on trail**. I should have had many lessons in an arena before venturing out on the trail.

2. **I didn't even know enough to pull back on the reins when the horse started to speed up** (and no one warned me that he always tried to speed up when he was pointed towards home).

3. **I was riding a "barn sour" horse** that was not suited for a novice rider.

4. **I had dropped the reins.** Split reins should always be tied in a knot for inexperienced riders because as a rule, beginners will usually drop the reins while grabbing for the saddle horn when panic sets in.

5. **I panicked and grabbed for the horn to try and hold on.** The saddle horn gives a false sense of security and actually works against you by keeping you from moving with the motion of the horse.

6. **I started screaming** thus scaring the horse more.

7. **I tried to jump off.** Warning: Do not try this at home! There are some cases where jumping off a horse is necessary. But for the most part, jumping off is not recommended.

Now that you clearly see what went wrong let me share with you my personal journey of how I moved out of this fear and into the joy of confident horsemanship. Let me first say that I am not a trainer. I am not an expert horsewoman. I haven't won any ribbons. But what I have accomplished is bigger than any titles, awards, or any accolades! What I have done is to overcome my fear of horses and have learned to ride with confidence. And for me, that is huge! I looked high and low for books, trainers and clinicians to give me the answers to help me overcome my fear. Don't get me wrong, many played a big part in getting me to the point where I am today but there was no quick fix, no step by step resource that I could draw on from the perspective of a non-trainer who just couldn't understand what I was going through. I am thoroughly convinced that one cannot fully understand this complex fear and thus help someone through it without having experienced it to the degree that it afflicted me. It is my hope that this book will help you learn from my experience and the experiences of those who were willing to share them with me so that you can overcome your fear and find the joy of fearless riding.

It is a miracle that I stuck with it. I think most people probably would have given up. Many people wondered why I continued to pursue it. I myself sometimes look back and marvel at my tenacity. But giving up never crossed my mind because I am a horse lover. I love everything about them and that love was stronger than my fear! Not having horses in my life simply was not an option. My husband lovingly calls it "an obsession". I prefer to call it "my passion". No, I would never give up. I would continue to seek out the secret to fearless riding; the secret of knowledge no matter how long it took!

Today I still continue to learn. In fact, I have found that I can never learn enough. My experience over the years has been that there are more people out there trying to ride horses without the basic know-how that they need than people out there who do know what they are doing. But the bigger problem is that a lot of the ignorant horse people in this world think they know everything there is to know about horses and don't try and listen to others to gain more knowledge. I personally know of many people who lack basic horsemanship skills who continually hop on their horses day after day and just hope for the best! That is no way to be for you or your horse. As far back as I can remember I wanted to learn to become a good horsewoman. It was the only thing I ever wanted to do.

When I was about 13, my grandparents had gotten to the age where they were no longer physically able to care for their ranch and their horses. So sadly, my horse fetish was put on hold. The occasional thrill of a rental pony was the only stimuli I had for many, many years. As a teenager, I continued to excel with my ballet training and I won many scholarships from major ballet companies and attended their summer programs in New York City. But my heart wasn't into ballet. I still longed to pursue my true love; horses! When I turned 18 years old, I broke the news to my parents that I knew would break their hearts but I also knew that I had to be true to myself. I did not want to become a ballerina. I didn't even like to dance! So after I came home from New York City the summer of my senior year in high school, I hung up my ballet shoes for good.

After graduating from college and getting married, my focus was on being a wife and raising my three sons. But it was in my early 30's that I began to dabble in the showing and raising of Miniature Horses. So once I became an adult I started out small (literally) and built on my passion from there.

When my children became more independent and I had the extra time, I purchased my first full-sized horse when I was about 39 years old. This was where both the fun and the frustration began and thus began my journey into the trial and error of overcoming my fear of the creatures I loved so much. I boarded my horses at many different types of facilities, both public and private, before my husband and I moved to a small ranch in North San Diego County and brought our horses to live at home with us.

My journey along the way (and while doing research for this book) led me to meet some very wonderful people that I am proud to call my friends. I will tell you what I learned and what worked for me as well as what has worked for some of my friends. I will share many stories, frustrations, and experiences as well as the advice from many noted experts that I had the pleasure to learn from. But most of all I will share with you the secret of my success: Which is K.I.C.K.

Keep at it! Don't give up.

Invest! Find a proper, well-trained horse and use solid well-made equipment.

Courage! It takes courage to face your fears and gain confidence.

Knowledge! Information needed to overcome the fear of the unknown.

I will break down these concepts and show you how to use knowledge and practical applications to K.I.C.K. your fear of horses. But in order for you to learn how to do this you will have to be truly honest. You will have to be truthful about your current level of horsemanship. You will have to put your excuses and rationalizations aside. No one knows more about this than me. I tried so hard to mask my fear that the dissection of it took extra long because I didn't want to admit it to anyone, let alone myself. I am not saying this task will be easy but if you are like me it will be one of the most worthwhile accomplishments of your life. And one thing is for sure; if I did it, so can you.

CHAPTER 1

Define Your Fear and Admit It!

I am sure that most people with horse fears have their own "Lopez" story of some kind or another. What happened to me during my first riding experience when I was a child shaped what I believed to be true about horses and instilled a deep foundation of fear. Without discounting your past experiences (because I'm sure they were very scary) I will attempt to help you separate fact from fiction. Because one must own up to their part in developing their fear and defining your fear is the first step. Ask yourself the following questions:

- **What is the source of your fear?** Do you have your own "Lopez" story? What was your role in exacerbating your incident? Is it what you don't know about horses? Is it what you *do* know and now are afraid of? Is it what you've been told about horses?

- **What exactly are you afraid of?** Are you afraid to ride a horse? Are you afraid on the ground? Are you afraid you can't control them? Do you just not know what to do around them? Are you afraid they will bite you or kick you?

- **How far back does your fear go?** Were you frightened by a horse as a child? Were you at one time a pretty good rider and an accident robbed you of your courage? Are you older now and afraid of being hurt? Why have you lost your confidence?

- **What are the physical symptoms of your fear?** Do you get sick to your stomach? Do your palms sweat? Do you get a lump in your throat? Does your heart pound?

Susan's Story

Accidents are a very real possibility when riding a horse. If you are being truly honest, most accidents are the fault of the rider. In fact, most people I have talked to that had a fear issue after having a riding accident have admitted that the incident occurred due to some fault of their own. Sometimes accidents are so traumatic that they instill a little voice that nags at us "I better not try that again". Therefore, many of us are never comfortable riding again and constantly worry about the next accident that *could* occur at any given moment. Sadly, some people never get on a horse again.

But there are other people that have had horseback riding accidents that have been able to overcome their fear. These successes will be examples to you as you read this book. Susan's story will demonstrate to you that first, and most importantly, you must own up to your part in what went wrong in the accident. Second, have a plan in place to avoid it ever happening again.

Susan is a mature and successful registered nurse. She is unassuming, kind and engaging towards everyone she meets. She is single and works in a hospital as an operating room nurse.

Her joy is her days off where she spends time with her horses at home on her ranch in Louisiana. Two separate incidents happened to her in a short period of time that had to do with mounting and dismounting that caused such a fear that it kept her from riding her horses for almost a year. Keep in mind that in the past, Susan would get on any horse at anytime with absolutely no fear.

As Susan has gotten older she has developed some limitations with regard to her mobility that requires her to mount and dismount slowly. She admitted that she felt that she needed to be careful since she had gotten older and had become a little overweight. Therefore, she needed a horse that would stand still and be patient while she got on and off. One day, while out on a trail ride with a few friends, Susan needed to dismount because she felt her saddle was loose and she wanted to get off and tighten the cinch. While dismounting, the saddle slipped and slid down to the horse's side which caused her to fall off and land on her shoulder and hip. She didn't think that she was hurt badly but her friends felt that she should walk back to the trailer while her friend ponied her horse. She was upset with herself because she realized that she had forgotten to check the cinch before she mounted.

Three days later while standing on a bucket trying to mount the same horse, Susan accidentally kicked her horse's rump while slinging her leg over his back and the horse suddenly bucked and sent her flying. She landed flat on her back and was in so much pain she couldn't move for a minute or two. Once she was able to get up she realized that she didn't have any broken bones but she was in excruciating pain for several weeks. Her back, her neck and every other muscle and bone in her body ached from the trauma of the fall. Her pain was enough to remind her over and over that 'if I get hurt again, maybe even worse next time, who's going to pay the bills if I can't work?' This is a valid concern that nagged at her so much that it kept her from getting back on a horse for over a year.

So how did she decide to get back on? First of all, she *wanted* to ride again. She loved it and she missed it. But it took courage! Lots of courage! She began by being honest about her part in her accidents. With the first fall, she admitted that she hadn't checked her cinch before she mounted. With the second fall, the horse hadn't been ridden since the first incident three days before and Susan was trying to mount, while still very sore, from a bucket that was not stable. Horses sense all kinds of emotions from us. They can feel it if we are apprehensive, weak, angry or nervous. So Susan's uneasiness made the horse feel on edge, which made him overreact to Susan's accidental kick to his rump upon mounting.

Susan now rides with confidence again. She attended a 6-day confidence building clinic and relearned basic horsemanship and reviewed the groundwork exercises. She learned to teach her horse not to walk off until she gave the okay. Once the horse did everything she had asked on the ground over and over, Susan was ready to mount. Only this time, Susan did not mount on a bucket or a fence rail. Susan purchased herself a sturdy mounting block and she asked a friend to hold her horse still while she mounted for the first few times. Realizing her part in contributing to her accident and therefore to her fear, Susan's fear began to melt away and her confidence slowly returned.

Start a Journal of your Journey

In order for you to start your journey to KICK your fear of horses, you must honestly admit and define your fear so that you can begin to work on changing it. I recommend writing your answers to the above questions down and elaborate with how ever much detail you need. Better yet, start a horse journal and jot down your journey into fearless horsemanship. Record helpful training notes as well as ideas and quotes that speak to you. Record your riding experiences both past and present and honestly look at your role in both what went wrong and what you've begun to do that has proven to be successful. Continue to write down all of your riding sessions as you begin this journey so that you can critique yourself as you begin to change. There is no better way to conquer fear than to face it and walk through it. This does take a lot of courage but if you are like me, your love of horses is well worth any discomfort you might experience along the way.

Admit It

Once I had started boarding my horse in a public stable that was only 10 minutes from my home, I would plan my work day around going to the barn and going for a ride. I would be excited to be going to see my horse but as the time grew closer and closer my palms would begin to sweat and I would get that jumpy hollow feeling in the pit of my stomach. By the time I arrived at the stable I would start to make excuses why I couldn't ride because I was so afraid. So I would end up visiting with my friends at the stable while just brushing my horse that day. One of my friends told me that she was journaling her horse progress. I remember thinking that was a great idea but looking back I now can see that I was not being honest about my fear in those days. My thoughts revolved around how I wished I could be a better rider and wondering why it wasn't happening to me. One of the reasons that it was not "happening" to me was that I had never been taught the importance or the techniques of proper ground work. This important step was completely skipped. I will go into proper ground work in a later chapter but as I look back in my early training days, I had no idea how to handle a horse on the ground. And on the days that I did ride my horse, I would be a so be a so nervous that

I would literally pray that nothing would spook my horse. Sound familiar? This is no way to go about enjoying your horse. Now that I have overcome my fear, one of the best perks of my new-found confidence is the joy of trail riding.

I have known people who have shown and ridden horses successfully for years and years that will never leave the security of the arena. There are many horse show participants and semi-professionals out there who have won many trophies and ribbons who miss out on the peaceful freedom of trail riding. I've known endurance riders who compete on a regular basis who are afraid to do more than a trot and never ask their horses to canter. Did you know that it takes more balance to ride your horse in a trot than a gallop? So you see you are not the Lone Ranger. You are just being honest by admitting you are afraid and are trying to do something about it. This is the first step to change.

I know it is not always easy to admit your fear. I see more fearful riders than confident ones and what they all have in common is their "appearance" which is to convince others as well as themselves that they are not afraid. Now I know sometimes admitting fear seems like you are succumbing to it which feels like you are making it worse in your mind. And many times when I admitted my fear to others, even trainers, I didn't get the results I was looking for; which was help. But actually admitting it to yourself and those around you is the first step in your commit-ment to change. My observation of the people, who won't admit their fear to others, is that they are the same ones who won't listen to sound advice about what they are doing wrong and this is actually contributing to their fear.

Stop Making Excuses

I had a friend who was very afraid of horseback riding (but of course tried to hide it) and when I would try to give her pointers here and there she always had an excuse. I would remind her to keep her heels down or to loosen up her reins and give her horse his head and she would reply with something like, "I don't feel like thinking about it now." or "I'm just relaxing today". Is it laziness or is it too much work to learn to ride correctly? Think about your excuses. What are they telling you? One thing I can attest to: Fear does not just *go away* one day by itself! It takes time, courage and tenacious effort…it takes K.I.C.K.! Remember?

Keep at it! - Means it takes practice and hard work.

Investment – in your time, effort, proper equipment and the proper horse

Courage to gain confidence.

Knowledge – Learning and listening to the advice of your teachers.

Another acquaintance I have ridden with in the past used to try and hide her fear of cantering her horse by exclaiming how smooth her horse's trot was. As with some gaited horses, there are exceptions to this rule but generally a normal Quarter Horse canter is much smoother than their trot. I haven't found an extended trot yet that I enjoy as much as a nice smooth rhythmic canter. But there she was holding her horse's reins too tight praying he wouldn't break into a canter!

But the excuse I liked the best (and have used myself) was that the horse was not *in the mood* to be ridden that day. I remember telling one of my trainers that I thought my horse was in pain so that I could get out of a particularly difficult lesson where my horse was not cooperating and it was requiring me to be very assertive with him (which was scary). "Why can't he just do this right?" I thought to myself. Just as in raising children, we know we are not to give in to their every whim so why do we do it with our horses? I just wished for every ride to go smooth but never wanted to deal with the scary work involved to be prepared if it didn't. I've used every excuse in the book so I can spot them a mile away. Ever hear the saying, 'you can't kid a kidder!?!' Well you can't hide fear from someone who's lived with it.

I am not sure why it is but it seems to me that the people that are the most fearful are the ones that are most resistant to help. It's as if they think that if they take your advice it will expose how much they don't know. So what? Stop acting as if you know everything and accept the tips from those that are in the position to help you. Obviously if you are reading this book you know that what you have been doing is not working. And month after month your riding is not improving and your fear isn't magically melting away. You sometimes even secretly ask yourself why you continue to ride when you don't really enjoy it.

Healthy Fear

Where fear robs us of our horse enjoyment I don't think being completely fearless is good either. The absence of a small amount of healthy fear can make us careless and can set us up for danger. I would be lying if I were to say that I don't have a small amount of fear left inside but this is what I call *healthy fear* or simply, *awareness*. If we are not alert and watching out for ourselves and our horse friends we could end up hurt. I still get a surge of adrenaline when my horse unexpectedly spooks or pulls back but as fast as it comes, it goes away. I no longer belabor and repeat the incident in my mind over and over and worry about the next time when this could happen again. This worry-free state of mind that I have been able to achieve has allowed me to soak up the pure enjoyment that my horse gives me on a daily basis both on the ground and in the saddle. This is an attainable goal that I also want for you. This is the joy that you can experience also.

What Kind Of Rider Do You Want To Be?

There is a huge difference between horseback riders and horsemen (or horsewomen). Ask yourself which do you aspire to be? Some horseback riders do not really have the time or the drive to be more than just that which is okay. Maybe horse owner-ship is not the best choice for them.

Horsemen are constantly trying to get inside the head of their horses to better become the true leader of the horses they ride. They strive for a partnership, a oneness, with their horses and won't rest until they have accomplished this.

CHAPTER 2

It's Not the Horse!

Once you've defined your fear and admitted it to yourself and anyone else who might be in the position to help you get over it, you now must acknowledge that most of the time the problem is not the horse, but in fact you! I bought and sold three horses before I found the two I have now because I kept thinking I wasn't choosing the right horse. In two of the cases, they probably weren't the right horse for me but the third one would have been fine had I known better what I was doing. I always wondered why other people could ride these horses with all the ease that I just could not master. "The horse just doesn't like me," I used to conclude. When in fact my lack of knowledge (and skill), my lack of understanding of the nature of horses, and of course, my fear was the true reason that I could not seem to bond with my horse. The poor horse would see me coming and begin to brace himself because I was this ball of negative emotions that had no leadership over him at all. No horse wants to "join up" with a rider that he can't trust.

The Nature of Horses

Horses, by nature, are very spiritual creatures. My hope is that more horse owners will truly understand this and thus experience this phenomenal trait. To experience the deep sensitivity of a horse is to experience being one with him. Their intuition and their ability to assess us humans can almost be scary. Your understanding of them is the key to building a relationship, a partnership and a bond with them. It is the key to overcoming your fear.

Horses are flight animals by nature. This means that they are always on the look out for danger. My friends and I joke about the evil rocks, bushes or monsters that are lurking in the dark shadows of our horse's minds. When a horse is out on trail his flight instinct is heightened even more. So by their very nature all horses are going to spook every now and then, especially when they are out on trail. You need to expect this (but not worry about it) and stop dreading it. We will go into this more with regards to how to deal with this in a later chapter. But for now understand that their flight instinct is not going to ever completely go away. How you react to it will make all the difference to your horse as he learns to trust in you as his rider and as you begin to build your confidence so that his occasional spooks won't concern you so much.

While there are exceptions to every rule, the average horse, by nature, is typically not trying to hurt you or anger you. When a horse "acts up" it is usually due to pain or fear. Try and remember this before you take their behavior so personally. I remember trying to get my horse to pick up his left lead and he kept refusing again and again. He started throwing his head and bouncing me around and my trainer declared, "He's just being an ass!" Since she was the authority at the time, I believed her and worked and worked until he finally picked up his left lead. A few days later this same horse was acting slightly lame and when it didn't go away, the vet came and blocked his left front heel and took x-rays. It turned out that his left front coffin joint had some inflammation and had to be injected with cortisone. He needed several weeks off to heal, so in fact my horse was not being an ass but was truly in pain.

The same goes for fear. When your horse spooks or acts up on trail he very well could sense what he perceives as possible danger that you simply are not tuned into. Horses use their sense of smell to help gage their comfort and guide their personal safety in any given situation. This is why horses seem spookier when the weather is windy. With all the scents that are whirling around in the wind, they simply can't get a good read on their surroundings. The only time my horse spooks or acts up is because of fear. He becomes startled if a dog runs around the corner unexpectedly, a bird (or butterfly) flies up in front of him, a branch has dropped from a tree, or even a shadow (sometimes his own) is lurking on the ground in front of him. This is normal horse behavior. If you are to overcome your fear you have to be realistic about what your expectations of your horse's behaviors are. Are you expecting too much? Are you thinking that you need a more 'bomb-proof' horse because yours spooks? Because you need to understand that while there are different degrees of horse bravery (mine is pretty much a chicken) *all horses spook* at one time or another. It is just their nature.

Horses Move Away From Pressure

We teach horses to move away from pressure. This is also a natural response for them. You press your left leg into their left side and they move to the right. So emphasizing this to them while we ride them is building upon proper ground work and what is also natural for them. Have you ever seen a horse jump towards what has startled them? Usually not. So if you fear that leading your horse on the ground will lead to their jumping on you, this is not common because it is not their nature. Again let me say that while there are exceptions to this rule (because there have been cases of unruly horses with very poor ground manners that have actually run over people) the norm is that a horse *typically* will not jump into you, in fact, he will try and avoid you at all cost.

Your Horse's Eyes

Look at your horse's eyes. What do you see? Do you see dark softness? Relaxed eyelids? Do you see the whites of his eyes? Do you see a wrinkle above his eye or are his eyes squinted? All of these things mean something. Obviously a soft dark eye with relaxed lids is a horse that is in a calm and relaxed state. Big and wild eyes and being able to see his whites mean he is nervous, anxious or scared. A "pig eye" is a mad eye that usually looks squinted or has a wrinkle above it like a lizard. Start to notice your horse's eyes more to get an understanding of how he is feeling in different situations. Jot it down in your horse journal as you observe what you see.

Your Horse's Ears

Now let's look at your horse's ears. I think we all know what pinned ears mean. This gives us a clear and concise warning into where our horse's brain is at. He is mad, annoyed or in pain! To avoid being hurt, heed the warning of pinned ears and get out of the way. If you are in the saddle, move away from the situation that your horse is annoyed with.

Another ear position that is very telling is when they are both perked forward. This usually means the horse is alert, curious or intent on something. When one ear is forward and the other is cocked sideways, this usually means he is listening to you or who ever is in the direction of his cocked ear. So take notice of his ears and jot down all of your observations in your horse journal. This will help you continue to understand your horse.

What Your Horse is Trying to Tell you.

Understanding your horse's nature as well as his body language will help you get a good read on him. Once you begin to understand what your horse is trying to tell you is when you can start to build a partnership with him. If you don't understand each other how do you expect to become a good and fearless rider? Remember your lack of understanding and knowledge adds to your sense of fear. When you understand that your horse is not trying to hurt you, is not trying to anger you, and is not intentionally trying to be an "ass" towards you, you can let go of some of the unknowns that contribute to your fear. It is not personal so stop making it that way. We, as horse owners, have a responsibility to try and understand our horses. This is how we begin to establish trust.

My friend Karen recently had an experience with her 30-year-old mare. Whistles clearly told her that she wanted to change her pasture mate. She had recently brought home her young show gelding named Vinny from a show barn. Whistles took an instant liking to this young horse. One day Karen went out to one of her pastures to bring in the horses for the night when she noticed that the old mare wouldn't come to the gate. She stood planted in one spot next to the fence near the young gelding in the next pasture over. At first Karen didn't think much of it and led in another horse first. When she came back to get the mare, she was still in the same place. Karen looked intently at the mare and thought to herself, "Does she want to be with Vinny?"

The next morning, Karen decided to put the mare in the pasture with Vinny and waited to make sure they would get along together. When the mare realized she was going to go in with the young gelding she began to prance. Karen could feel her mare's pleasure and satisfaction with being understood. "If I hadn't been listening to her, I could have missed what she wanted." The two horses never once squealed or even attempted to act like they needed to get to know each other. Instead, they happily began to graze side by side as if they had been pasture mates all of their lives. Karen stated to me, "I wish people would just leave their egos at home and stop and listen to what their horses are trying to tell them." To drive home the importance of understanding your horse better, read on about the undeniable scientific facts that a very famous veterinarian has documented in his work.

Unlocking the Secrets of Horse Behavior

Recently I had the pleasure of meeting Dr. Robert M. Miller who is a well-known equine veterinarian and expert on horse behavior. He has written several books on both subjects and explained to me the importance of understanding horse behavior. He has written an entire book on the subject entitled "Understanding the Ancient Secrets of the Horse's Mind". He also has a DVD called "Understanding Horses" that goes into even greater detail about how to apply this knowledge to problem solving. I encourage everyone to read his book or watch his DVD, but until you do, he has allowed me to summarize these 10 important behaviors here for you to use as a tool for better understanding the mind of your horse. As you read these 10 behaviors use your horse journal to ask yourself how these facts relate to your fear:

1. **Horses Are Flight Animals:** This fact is why we have so many problems with horses. Simply, horses are programmed to run away from what they fear. As I mentioned earlier, their flight instinct is the behavior that helps them navigate their surroundings to measure their safety.

2. **Horses Are the Most Perceptive of All Domestic Animals:** Their hearing is beyond the range of the human ear as well as their sense of smell. The most sensitive area of a horse is their mouth and their sense of touch is very refined. They have stereoscopic binocular vision which means that they can see 360 degrees. However, they have little to no depth-perception.

3. **Horses Have the Fastest Response Time of Any Domestic Animal:** Again, being flight animals, horses must be able to run away instantly from danger. They are the fastest runner of any domestic species.

4. **Horses Are Able to Desensitize Quickly to Frightening Stimuli:** You can easily teach a horse not to fear harmless things quickly. Let them examine what they are afraid of and soon curiosity will replace fear.

5. **Horses Are Fast Learners:** They are very intelligent animals and are able to learn at great speed and remember what they learned.

6. **Horses Have Fantastic Memories:** Horses never forget anything and significant experiences, good or bad, are emblazoned into their memory forever. Fortunately, horses are very forgiving and constantly try to understand what we are trying to communicate to them. Bad experiences naturally cause horses to want to flee.

7.   **Horses Are Herd Animals:** Horses naturally live by a pecking order or "dominance hierarchy". Horses look for leadership. If we are effective, we can become our horse's leader.

8.   **Horses Use Positional Control of Movement:** Positional control is the way a horse establishes leadership. Control of movement is the basis of all horse training because horses accept our dominance when we ask them to move when they would rather not.

9.   **Horses Display Distinct Body Language:** Licking his lips, swishing his tail, throwing his head; all of these things mean that your horse is trying to communicate something to you. We, as horse owners, need to observe, listen and heed what our horses are trying to tell us.

10. **Horses Are A Precocial Species:** Precocity means that they are self-sufficient at birth. Their brains are fully formed and they are usually up on their feet within one hour after they are born. To my surprise, Dr. Miller said that the horse's prime learning period in their life is from birth to the first two weeks of life. Does that statement shock anyone else? Many horses go untouched during that time yet that is when we should be teaching them to lead, to pick up their feet, to getting accustomed to having their ears touched, even clipped, and their mouth opened just to name a few.

If we all understood how sensitive and intuitive our horses are, we would experience them in a whole different dimension; one that would forever change the relationship and understanding between humans and horses.

CHAPTER 3

K . I . C . K .

Keep At It!

One of the most important aspects of learning how to K.I.C.K. your fear of horses is to *Keep At It*! Don't give up! This is a big reason that I was finally able to overcome my fear. I went to trainer after trainer and shelled out a lot of money trying to learn to be a good rider but my fear kept me from being able to organize the knowledge I was getting and put it into action. But I never gave up. I kept at it until I finally got it! Keeping at it requires a substantial investment of your time. Lessons and time in the saddle are the secret. Maybe you should not buy a horse if you can only ride him on the weekends. Horses *need* to be ridden. Horses *love* to be ridden. Having them sit in a stall all week makes them bored, lazy, and barn sour which quickly removes their drive to want to be worked. It's just like people trying to exercise and stay in shape. Once we get off the couch and into a work-out routine we feel good. But once we stop working out we get lazy. The same goes for horses. My horses get out everyday of the week even if it is just a turnout or to be brushed. So making time for lessons and riding at least three days a week is what your horse needs and is what it takes to learn so that you can overcome your fear.

Along my journey I went to four different trainers as well as attending two week-long horsemanship clinics in another state. I did gain some knowledge with each experience, some more than others, but my fear was still there. I finally found someone who was able to pull all of this knowledge together in terms that I could understand. This process, this search, took more than seven years. Now I am not saying this is the norm or how long it will take you but the point is; I did not stop searching and I did not give up. Neither should you. So **K**eep at it!

Invest in the Right Horse

My "Lopez" experience instilled in me a strong belief that horses were big and powerful and that they could hurt me. I tried to mask my fear but every time I was around horses my body language told the real story…that I was pensive and scared. But again, my passion was stronger than my fear which is what kept me at it. I have a sneaking suspicion that is what has kept you at it also. As an adult, I was not only worried about every possible spook while I was in the saddle but I felt extremely vulnerable on the ground standing next to a horse as well. I just didn't know how to handle them and without the proper knowledge it was just hit or miss with the hope that I did not get in their way.

When I got my first horse I boarded him at my friend's ranch which was about an hour drive from my home. Nicki is my good friend and was willing to charge me only what her costs were for board. Since money was a consideration, the long distance seemed like a small price to pay to finally get to have a horse of my own. Nicki only had mares at the time so she encouraged me to look for a mare also. I purchased Dusty as a 6-year-old. She was a beautiful red roan Quarter Horse out of the famous stallion Impressive. She also was HYPP positive/negative. What?

I had no idea what this meant. Her previous owner never told me anything about it until he trailered her over to Nicki's ranch. When he was leaving he casually mentioned, "Oh by the way she can't eat alfalfa" and handed me a copy of an article out of a horse magazine that explained this puzzling disease that had been genetically traced back to the breeding stallion named Impressive. Without getting off the subject and into complexities of HYPP let me just say that I was fortunate she never had an "episode" when I owned her (where she could collapse and possibly have a seizure). But the problem was that she didn't like grass hays and seeing the other horses around her eating alfalfa made her feel like she was missing something, which made her very cranky!

It was with Dusty that I learned that horses could "cow kick"! I was always told that you should never walk behind a horse because they could kick you. But no one ever told me that they could kick out to the side. She was terribly irritable when she was being saddled and it didn't help that she was very "cinchy" (sensitive when you'd tighten her cinch belt underneath her girth). She'd put her ears back, try to bite me, and swish her tail while I would try and keep far enough away for her not to cow kick me. Her attitude only made my fear worse. I bought several different saddles and pads trying to figure out what her problem was until finally I was just too afraid to ride her anymore. I made excuses to Nicki that I was too busy to come and ride Dusty until she suggested that maybe I should get riding lessons.

I found a trainer from an ad in the paper and she told me right away to get rid of Dusty and, of course, buy a horse from her. Now some people have a hard time making the decision to sell a horse that is not a good match for them. It makes them feel like they failed. Try not to get caught up with that self-defeating guilt. It will be very hard for you to get over your fear if you are not matched up with the right horse. So she sold me a supposedly "really broke" paint horse that she had just picked up at a local auction named Apache. He started out to be fine until the drugs wore off (yes I do believe he was sedated) and exactly three weeks after I got him, he was a different horse than I had purchased. (A simple blood test could have detected this at a pre-purchase exam.) He absolutely would not tolerate having his ears touched and would freak out, pull back and break his lead rope and run off if you did. He did this many, many times and broke many, many halters and lead ropes. Since you could not put the bridle over his ears, you had to unbuckle the headstall and put it on him like you would a halter while trying to hold the bit in his mouth. One day out on trail and for no apparent reason that I could explain, he started spinning like a reining horse until the law of gravity took over and I was flung off his back like a rag doll. Needless to say, Apache was not a participant in helping me overcome my fear. A good trainer might have been able to help this horse with his issues but he was not a good horse for a novice rider with fear issues.

My third horse purchase was a 7-year-old ranch-broke gelding that was a cross between a Mustang and a Quarter Horse. Gideon was a stout buckskin gelding with a sweet and gentle disposition. Knowing what I know now, I wish I had never sold him. But Gideon didn't have a chance with me. Too many other bad experiences before him had robbed me of any courage I had to give him a fair shake. I thought he was too spooky and he truly was. But it was because I was such a nervous wreck! Horses look to their rider for the encouragement they need to be brave and Gideon never got any from me. Eventually yet another trainer advised me to sell him and get a more suited horse for me to "show".

My quest for Chief began after I had started with this new trainer who primarily showed Western Pleasure. She was just beginning to merge into reining and was advising all of her clients to start buying reining horses. Most of us did. Being that

Gideon was a non-registered ranch horse, this trainer advised me to sell him and look for a more appropriate show horse. It was clear from the get go that I could not afford an already-trained finished reining horse. So she had this brilliant idea that I should buy an untrained baby and she would train him to rein and in a couple of years I would have a finished reiner! Right? Wrong! A novice rider should never purchase a novice horse. But this trainer had her own agenda in mind rather than my best interest. Shortly after the purchase, she was subsequently fired from the stable I was boarding at, but what was done was done, which was just the beginning of my journey with Chief.

Anyway, I bought Spectacular Cheifton. He was a beautiful, loud, black and white Tobiano colt that grew and grew and grew until it was obvious that he would never become a reiner. Today he stands at 16.1 hands and I've since found out that his father was a world champion roping horse (Range Cheifton) as was his grandfather (Hank A Cheifton) and were not champion reining horses like I was led to believe. I'll get more into the trials and tribulations of training Chief in a later chapter but let me just say that he was never easy in any sense of the word and even now, though he knows his job, he still makes me work for it. I would not recommend this experience to a novice or someone with fear issues and even though, after many years, it eventually worked itself out for me (because I was willing to 'Keep At It!'). It was a long and frustrating haul! I am telling you all of this so that you might learn from my mistakes. Cheap horse after cheap horse purchase finally taught me that if I wanted the right horse for myself, I would have to pay for it. Well-trained horses don't come cheap! I recently heard Clinton Anderson say that the problem today is that there are too many horses out there that are over bred, overfed, under trained and under ridden. Once again, let me emphasize, if you are not willing to learn the proper skills and put in the time, you are better off not owning a horse.

When beginning your search for the right horse you must first decide what kind of horse you want. Base this decision on what you want to do with your horse. If you want to show, obviously you would look for a horse that is trained in the particular discipline that you want to do. If you are just looking for a good trail horse then start there. Many years ago when my husband wanted to learn to ride with me (God bless him) I had finally learned what qualities to look for in a horse for a beginner rider. I searched and searched until I finally found a well-trained 8-year-old Quarter Horse bay gelding, Poco's Heaven Sent, or simply, "Cody". He is the kind of horse that I wish everyone could have the pleasure of owning. He is the definition of gentle; which is quiet (relaxed), kind and well-trained. He is truly a *once-in-a-life-time-horse!* I call him "The Cadillac" because he knows his job and once you get on him you just put him in 'drive' and go. Cody's purchase price was $7500.00. I mention this because cheaper horses usually mean they lack in training and we must remember the old saying "you get what you pay for!"

Being partial to geldings and the even-temperedness of Quarter Horses I began my search there. I ruled out other breeds and mares and any horse under the age of seven. I looked for a soft eye, a gentle willing spirit, and good training. Again, these qualities don't come cheap. Remember the initial purchase of your horse will be the cheapest part of your investment. I feel sorry for people who get the "free" horses thinking that they made out so great. I guarantee they don't end up being free regardless of the absence of the purchase price. There is usually a reason if a horse is free. You end up paying at some time or another whether it is in training or in veterinary bills. The scariest decision that I have heard many times before, is the inexperienced rider who get their *practically free* horses "off the track". Beginners and people with fear issues have no business owning this type of horse. Yes, they are usually low-priced or free but the road to overcoming fear will be long and frustrating with a horse that has been bred for speed. Remember, that the training for your horse is not going to be cheap. Another pit fall can also be getting a rescued horse. Rescued or abused horses are considered "special need" horses and unless you have the skill set to handle them, they are not a good choice for novice riders or riders with fear issues.

I recently heard about a woman in her 60's who had always wanted a horse for herself and for her young granddaughter to ride. She basically knew very little about horses and I don't think she did much riding even when she was younger. Now if you have been paying attention so far you have learned that lack of knowledge about horse's often can lead to uneasiness around them which then can lead to fear. So against the advice of everyone she asked, who had the knowledge to help her, she went ahead and bought a 14-year-old Thoroughbred mare that came from the race track. Apparently she was a relatively sweet mare but was nonetheless a high-spirited horse that was bred for speed. This woman was attracted by her beauty, her low-price of $2000.00 and the "sweet" fact that the mare used her teeth to untie the woman's shoe. Last time I checked, the horse had thrown the woman who then never rode her again and was being boarded in the backyard of her friend's house, was not being ridden by anyone, but was being brushed a lot and showered with tons of carrots and lots of affection. Does this sound like it is a match made in heaven? No, this has potential for being a recipe for disaster!

If I could have back just half of the money I wasted by buying the wrong horses, the wrong equipment, and in bad trainers I could probably retire. Owning horses is never cheap. So if you cannot afford to buy a well-trained horse that is right for you wait until you can. An under-trained horse will not lessen your fear, but will simply make your fear worse. There is an old joke that goes something like, "Do you know how to make a million dollars in horses?...Start with 10 million!" This is so true! So give yourself a realistic budget because horses with good dispositions and good training aren't inexpensive!

Well-known radio/television host and author, Rick Lamb recommends taking someone with you that has good horse skills and experience to help you evaluate if the horse that you are thinking of buying is a good match for you. Rick gives a very good talk called "Finding Flicka" where he gives some very good tips for seeking out the best matched horse for your skill set and personality. Once you find a horse that you are interested in buying, he recommends taking a "surprise visit" to see the horse again. "When you show up unannounced the seller has not had the time to 'work down' the horse or prepare him for your visit," Rick said. "While you must be respectful of the seller's privacy, this is a great way to get a more accurate read on the horse for what he truly is."

Remember that buying a young or "green" horse is never a good idea. Rick explained that many "green" riders make this mistake due to a cheaper initial purchase price or the notion that both horse and rider will "learn together". This was my logic. So please listen and learn from my mistake, this is not a good decision and will set you up for a lot of frustration and certainly will not help you with your fear. He further explained that since we get dogs and cats as babies, people can sometimes think this is the way it is done with horses also. But, in fact, the opposite is true. "The less experience you have," Rick said, "The more experience the horse should have." The older, tried and true horse is always a great choice but remember to have a vet check out any horse you are thinking of purchasing.

You might have guessed that the first few horses that I bought on the word and expertise of others, I did not have vet checked. With the first two of them I could have benefited from that information and probably would have passed on buying those horses. So learn from me, pay a trainer that you trust to go with you and ride the horse you are thinking of buying and remember to always get a vet check. These are cheap investments that could avoid expensive disasters down the road. Broke horses priced at $2500.00 are priced low for a reason. Whereas you might find someone who is selling cheap because of the recent downturn in the economy, most sellers with good horses know what they have and will wait for the price of what their horses are truly worth. So "buyer beware" and *beware* of horse traders. Because horse traders don't care what kind of rider you are or what kind of horse you are looking for they will try and sell you anything. I know this first hand!

Invest in the Proper Equipment

Another important aspect of achieving successful horse experiences is investing in good equipment. The proper equipment makes for a happy horse. Forget gimmicks! Whether it is saddles, bits or whatever else someone came up with to convince you to give up your money, always go with the tried and true! I don't ride English so I can only advise you on Western equipment. But handmade leather saddles with genuine lambs wool padding and solid rawhide full quarter trees have been what the professionals have used for years. There is a reason that they are still around and are still the best bet for you and your horse. Proper saddle fitting is probably the second most important decision you'll make after you've selected the proper horse. It requires an expert eye to make the right choice. Your trainer, veterinarian, or a saddle-fitting expert should be able to help you with this. Most people will let you try a saddle before making you pay for it. Good saddles are also not cheap, so if money is an issue, look for a used one that is handmade. Well-made saddles are designed to last for 30 years or more so a used 10-year-old saddle is just getting broken-in! Even if you have to replace the seat and padding or do other small repairs, it is well worth it if you find a nice used one.

As far as bits go, I have a drawer full of them. All purchased and tried on the bad advice of people who supposedly knew more than I did. Now I am not a trainer so I am not going to attempt to tell you what bit you should use for your horse (seek the advice of a professional trainer) but I will tell you that bits should not be gimmicky or complicated. And the one thing I do know is that you should make sure that you get a bit made of sweet iron, copper or the type of metal that "browns" which looks like rust. Shiny metallic bits don't taste good to horses. In fact, they annoy them. Ever bite down on aluminum foil? If you have, you know the feeling I am talking about. A bit that "browns" tastes good to horses and encourages their mouth to make more saliva. This is what you want to happen when you are riding your horse.

Courage to Gain Confidence

"Courage is being scared to death but saddling up anyway."
–John Wayne

If you want to gain confidence around horses you have to have courage! Courage, simply, is being afraid but forcing yourself to do what you are afraid of anyway. Courage is not an emotion, it is an action! And it takes courage to stare your fear in the face! You must continually walk through your fear if you are going to conquer it. You must be brave!

Now I am not a daredevil. I have no aspirations to climb mountains, sky dive, or do anything else that is considered "thrill seeking" but where horses are concerned I have courage. My love for them was stronger than my fear. I remember on one particular day during a colt breaking clinic I attended, four of us (two men and two women) had to literally gentle, saddle and ride for the first time, a two-year-old quarter horse. My palms started sweating as they led the unruly young horse out of his pasture and into the round pen. After sending him around the round pen for quite awhile and adequately gaining his respect and attention, we took turns gentling him, rubbing him all over with the pad, and slipping a rope around his girth to ready him for the cinch. The other woman in the clinic put the pad on his back and then I was instructed to place the 30 lb. saddle on him for the very first time.

I carefully hoisted the saddle up as gently on his back as I could to which he immediately exploded into a fit of bucking, running and carrying on. The saddle flew off and landed in the mud and I remember that all I was trying to do was to stay out of his way. Now, without courage, I would have run out of that round pen and been done with this nonsense. But courage kept me at it; courage and peer pressure. I couldn't let my clinic-mates see how scared I was. So I went over and picked up the muddy saddle and began to work at putting it on him again. This time, to my surprise, he didn't move. I will never forget the sheer terror I felt when I had to reach under his belly and grab the cinch. I slowly threaded the leather latigo through the D-ring of the cinch and gently began to tighten it. All the while in the back of my mind I knew this young colt could explode again at any given minute.

Within an hour we had all gotten this colt to the point where he was ready to be ridden. I watched him buck with the other riders, some more than others, and I remember when my turn came I just wanted throw up. I was terrified and I'm sure that everybody there knew it. But no one let me give up, they expected me to do it and since everyone else had done it, I rode him too. This, my friend, is called courage. This is when the act or accomplishment becomes more important than your fear.

Without courage you will never gain the confidence you need to overcome your fear. And confidence is gained with knowledge!

Knowledge

This is the topic where we need to spend most of our time and most of the remaining chapters will provide you with a lot of hints that will help you expand your knowledge. Since fear is being afraid of the unknown, having knowledge about horses will deliver you from much of your fear. And having good teachers is the key to gaining knowledge. I speak from experience when I say that not all trainers are good teachers! One does not need any credentials to nail up a shingle, call themselves a trainer, and take your money. Hopefully you will not have to search high and low for a good teacher as I did because my journey proved just how frustrating trying to learn can be.

In my experience many of the trainers threw too much at me at once. I remember the frustration of hearing them fire commands at me one after another that I didn't even understand. "Sit on your pockets!" "Don't let him dive in!" "Pick up his shoulder!" "Rock your hips!" How are you supposed to do these things when you don't know what they mean? How does one pick up a horse's shoulder? I can remember my head swimming with meaningless instructions and all the while my fear was still glaring at me in the face. In my opinion you must start from the beginning and master one aspect of proper riding at a time. Once, and only once, you have mastered that aspect should you move on to the next step. For example, begin by learning proper posture and where your proper seat should be in the saddle. Once sitting in that position becomes second nature to you (meaning you no longer have to think about it) then you can move on to mastering proper foot placement in the stirrups. Once you have that planted firmly in your brain you can move on to the next step. This method worked for me but it took a lot of practice in the arena between lessons. Trainers assume we understand their "lingo" but even though it makes sense to me now and I did finally master these things there was a time when it was all just words.

I had one trainer who noticed that I was not using my spurs correctly. I was jabbing the horse in his side instead of rolling the spur up under his belly. So instead of teaching me how to use them properly she had me go out and buy "ball" spurs so my jabbing wouldn't annoy the horse as much. I later learned that spurs are a tool not a weapon and it is important to learn how to use them properly. It was frustrating when every trainer I went to told me I was leaning too far forward in the saddle but none of them explained to me how to fix it (other than to lean back to which I just popped forward again).

That is until I finally found the teacher I had been searching for. She actually was not a professional trainer but she should have been! She was a friend and a neighbor who offered to help me with my young horse when we first moved to our own horse-zoned property. She was raised around horses; in fact her mother *was* a trainer. So from a very young age she rode English and showed Hunter/Jumpers. In her adult years she decided to "try" Western riding. I emphasis the word *try* because she ended up earning the prestigious title of "Rookie of the Year" in only her second year of showing reining horses. Carolyn Trammell can not only ride well but this gal can teach! She was able to explain to me in a way that made so much sense so that I could understand what I had to do to become a better rider. Under her tutelage and for the first time, all of the pieces to the puzzle began to come together for me.

All of the commands that all of the other trainers were telling me to do, she actually *showed me how to do*! Things started making sense as I began to understand my proper seat, my proper leg and foot placement, correct posture, where my hands should be, etc.

I even learned how to support the horse's shoulder and hips to keep him square! The key for me was the understanding of *why* all of these things were important for proper riding. My constant practice between lessons helped begin to train my brain to "feel" if I was riding correctly. After several months I noticed I no longer had to think about everything all the time, the parts were coming together naturally. I can't tell you how great it felt to finally "get it"! I remember my "aha" moment was when Carolyn asked me to canter my horse with a loose rein out on trail. Her confidence in my ability to do this made me feel like I could at least attempt it. To my amazement, my horse did not try and run away with me as I had feared, but rather loped along gently and stopped when I sat down in the saddle and said, "Whoa". It was then that I started to trust my ability to control my horse and begin to ride with confidence.

But don't ever think that all of this proper training came easy. It did not. It took commitment, hard work, and a lot of time (almost a year of two lessons per week). There were many days I just wanted my lesson to be over with because the frustration was overwhelming but I was not allowed to give up. Carolyn pushed me beyond where I ever thought I could go. And even when I didn't think I could do anymore, she pushed me even further. What I learned from this is that you cannot progress until someone pushes you outside of your comfort zone. And many people never will venture beyond that and therefore never will progress. So if you are to overcome your fear, you are going to experience discomfort at some level. I guarantee it. But if you want to become a good rider and get beyond the grips of fear you have to find a teacher who will gently push you beyond where you ever thought you'd be willing to go. So finding a good teacher that can actually teach you what to do, why you do it, and will push you beyond your comfort zone to see to it that you master it is the answer to the knowledge that you are seeking.

My mentor, Carolyn Trammell

CHAPTER 4

Continue to Learn and Grow!

I don't think that most people will ever really know everything there is about horses because just when you think you do, they teach you just how much you don't know. So I believe you must constantly be trying to learn more. An English dressage horse trainer friend of mine who has been training for over 30 years said that there are always new challenges with some of the horses she trains and it never ceases to amaze her. "They are always teaching me something new!" she said. Becoming a good and fearless rider takes skill. You don't just take a few lessons and think you're good to go. You must continue to perfect your craft for years to come. Interestingly enough the only time I almost gave up on the lessons was just before *I got it*! I was just cresting the mountain of understanding and I almost turned back. Again I say; don't give up! In many cases it is "darkest before the dawn" just as it was with me.

The old saying, "ignorance is bliss" is so true. Some people want to stay where they are because to progress means more responsibility for one's actions. Once I got into more advanced horsemanship is when it became more complex for me. I remember thinking, "no one ever told me this before" to which I realized that I had never gotten advanced enough to get to the point where any of it would have made sense. When my riding progressed I started to learn to collect my horse and support his shoulders and hips so that he stayed square between my legs. I had to learn to ask him to lift his belly and push his back up into the saddle and to propel himself with his back legs. It takes a good teacher to help you understand how to do this and why. You don't want to ride your horse all strung out. Strung out horses hold their heads up high in the air, hallow their back, and reach with their front legs. Collection is a very important key to proper horsemanship and this is the point where many people quit learning because it becomes harder and they think they've already learned enough to get by because after all, 'I only want to trail ride so I don't really need my horse to know this or I don't need to know that'. This is simply not true. In fact many times trail riding requires more skill due to all of the different obstacles and distractions that a rider can encounter in an uncontrolled environment.

Good Teachers and Bad Teachers

Remember, finding a good teacher is the key. I'll say it again; there are a lot of good horse trainers out there that are not good teachers. There is an art to teaching. Not all really smart experts in their field have the gift to teach their craft to others. You have to pick and choose. Sadly, there are some lousy trainers out there that give good trainers a bad name. It was unfortunate for me that I seemed to keep coming in contact with some not-so-great ones. So if you feel your trainer is not helping you, find another one.

I remember an incident I had after leaving one trainer and starting with another. I was having trouble with my young horse Chief and had reprimanded my him severely as the last trainer had taught me and when the new trainer saw this she went nuts and told me never to treat a horse like that (she was right but I was just doing what I had been taught before). I was forbidden from riding my horse for a few weeks until she felt I understood how to properly correct my horse. While this was correct to teach me this, she went overboard. She became the gatekeeper of whether or not I could ride my own horse. All of her decisions became *the only* decisions with regards to my horse. I was relegated to being just the writer of the checks! Have you ever had your trainer tell you when you're about to mount your horse, "I just got him right so don't wreck him"? This is yet another example of when it is time for you to move on.

As I mentioned earlier, I took lessons from at least four trainers before I found one that finally put it all together for me. Whereas I did learn a little something from all of them, I could never figure out why lesson after lesson I didn't feel like I was progressing. Many of my "horse friends" (using the same trainer) weren't that skilled either and had been with this trainer for many more years than I had. So what was wrong? Sometimes it is the old law of supply and demand. I think that some trainers are afraid that if they teach you everything they know you simply won't need them anymore. My English trainer friend told me that she has heard some of her colleagues refer to their clients as "mushrooms". "Keep them in the dark and feed them shit!" These were their words, not mine. Now let me say that while there are a few trainers out there that lack scruples there are many honest and integral trainers too. You just have to find them. Get referrals from a person who's riding skills you admire. Find out who taught them. Ask questions.

I remember taking "trail-riding" lessons from a trainer for over a year but after all of that time I still had no basic horsemanship skills. When I look back I can see now that we skipped a lot of the necessary steps. I was still on edge and afraid my horse would spook any minute and I had no concrete techniques for what to do if he did. She just used to tell me to "hold on". Hold on? Once you understand how to control your horse even under scariest of conditions your fear will melt away. I no longer ride with a chorus of "what ifs" playing continuously in my head. And I have to say there is no feeling in the world like riding my horses without fear. This was achieved by understanding, knowledge, and practical skills.

You too must learn why certain skills are necessary and how to achieve them. I am convinced that there are more people out there trying to ride horses, that lack the basic skills, than there are people who know what they are doing. Don't be one of the "skill-less know-it-alls" that can't be taught anything. You know who you are! You are the people who need more knowledge and rarely listen to those who are in the position to give it to you. You ignore any outside advice that could really help you and you could be setting yourselves and the people around you up for serious danger. Find a good professional!

New Research

And remember, equine research has developed significantly over the past few years which has dramatically improved our understanding of horses. More understanding of veterinary medicine, proper feed and nutrition, equipment, and training have come leaps and bounds to benefit the world of horses. Just because that is the way you did things when you were a kid does not mean it is the best way to do things today.

I have a distant neighbor who has two unruly "family" trail horses. Neither one has had the training necessary for him to be putting his novice wife and young children on them. One is even off the track but I'm sure the low price tags justified his decision to purchase these horses. In a casual conversation one day I asked him what he was feeding his horses to which he replied, "alfalfa". I asked him "why" to which I got an indignant response of "why not!?!" I explained that his horses weren't performance horses and recent studies showed that feeding alfalfa was not only not a good nutritional choice but that it basically was like feeding them rocket fuel. He tersely told me that he had been raised around Thoroughbreds and that is what they were fed 40 years ago and that it was still fine now.

Not always! According to an article entitled "A Horse Of Course" by Don Blazer, research has revealed that alfalfa was originally designed to be used as cattle feed and caught on as feed for horses particularly on the West Coast where it grew plentifully. Along with too much calcium and being low in phosphorus, alfalfa is far too high in protein which causes a horse's digestive system to have to work extra hard to convert the protein into usable energy which creates a high body temperature. This is where the term "hot" comes from. Horses that don't work hard everyday can't burn off enough of this protein and therefore become hyper or "hot". Grass hays are a much better choice for non-performance horses or trail horses that are just used for pleasure. I feed Timothy and Bermuda grass. Orchard grass is another good choice. It is important to keep up on the new findings within the horse world. While you don't want to jump on every new band wagon that comes by, you should be open to new research.

This same neighbor recently was on a trail ride with his wife when one of the horses spooked which freaked out the other one. His novice wife, not having the skills she needed to handle her horse, panicked and jumped off which resulted in several broken ribs, a collapsed lung and various other problems that landed her in ICU for many days. Now I am not saying that the alfalfa they fed caused this accident but I am saying that it probably didn't help. Neither did having the wrong horse and an inexperienced rider without the skill level to handle what was probably a very preventable accident.

Clinicians

Much like trainers, there are many good clinicians out there, some better than others. In my search for a good one I read many books, watched many videos, and observed many demonstrations until I found a clinician that I could identify with. I wanted to learn to be confident and many clinicians boast that they can build your confidence if you follow their methods but the key is to find the method that works for you and your horse. Richard Winters told me that most of his clinics turn into confidence building clinics. Try not to become a clinician "groupy" or clinician "hopper". These people go from clinician to clinican taking one program after another in hopes of achieving the confidence that they are looking for. The problem lies with implementing what you learned at the clinic to your horses when you get back home. This is why I think it is important to take your own horse to the clinic with you if at all possible.

My philosophy has always been K.I.S.S. – Keep It Simple Stupid! I didn't want to be more confused than I already was so I looked for common sense and simplicity. So many clinicians use too many obscure terms, special equipment, and unexplainable mystique for my taste. By that I mean they make it appear easy with all of their own tools and techniques but they can't seem to teach what they do to the average person to implement it once they get home. It is so amazing and inspiring to watch a good clinician gentle an unruly horse within a few minutes right before your very eyes. But the question is; can they show *you* how to do it? And if so, how long does it take? My first clinic was in 2002 with Chris Cox.

After watching his video on how he gentled a wild BLM mustang, I was so inspired that I was moved to tears. This wild horse was so frightened of humans that he quivered from his head to his tail and the sweat just poured off of him. Within minutes he allowed Chris to get close enough to touch him and within an hour he trusted Chris enough to relax and lie down, let Chris sit on him and pet him. All this was done by calmly teaching the horse trust and respect. Chris kept saying, "You make the right things easy and wrong things hard". He would reward even the slightest try to build the trust between himself and the horse by releasing the pressure. His methods didn't seem complicated but made complete sense as he explained his techniques as he went along.

I lost no time in contacting Chris regarding his week-long horsemanship clinics at his ranch in Mineral Wells, Texas. I arranged to attend a clinic a couple of months later. It was during this time that I had just purchased my young colt, Chief and since my current trainer had just been fired by the stable that I was boarding at, I didn't have any prospects for who was going to start training Chief. It was then that I got an idea. It was a long-shot, but what did I have to lose?

Would Chris Cox be willing to start Chief? "Probably not," I told myself, "but it couldn't hurt to ask!" So I called him back and asked him. "Well I don't usually do that," he answered, "But I just happen to have the time right now." I couldn't believe my ears. Had Chris Cox just agreed to start Chief's training? So after sorting out the details, I sent Chief off in a trailer the following week to spend the next few months in training with Chris.

Chris Cox working in the round pen with Chief.

Chris Cox riding Chief as a two-year-old colt.

CHAPTER 5

Learning About Yourself!

The Beginning of My Journey with Chris Cox!

Three weeks later I was on a plane headed for Texas. I met up with seven other people from various parts of the country with various different reasons for wanting to attend Chris' clinic. Some had more horse experience than I had and some had less. But the one thing we all had in common was a burning desire to become better riders.

The first couple of days we learned just how important ground work was. This was a concept that I had totally skipped; a huge hole in my efforts to become a better rider. No one had ever even told me, let alone taught me, about ground work. But if you think about it, it makes complete sense since we spend more time on the ground with our horses than on their backs. In fact, we didn't get on the back of a horse until the third day. The one thing that I quickly realized was that I was more comfortable on the back of a horse than I was on the ground next to him. All of this ground work terrified me! We had to learn the importance of disengaging the horse's hind quarters to learn to control him from his hips. You simply can't control a 1000 lb. horse by trying to pull on his head. You must learn to control him by moving his

hindquarters. We did exercise after exercise to test our understanding of our control over the horse on the ground. One of
the exercises required us to direct our horse over a log and have
him turn and face us. I remember when it came to my turn, I was
frozen with fear. I simply didn't think I could stand there and ask
a horse to jump over a log and have him turn and face me. I tried
a couple of times to which the horse simply ran around the log.
Frustration and defeat overwhelmed any sense of confidence I
had left. Chris did not relent. He expected me to do it and did
not move on until I did. My heart was in my throat and my mind
whirled with Chris' incomprehensible voice commands. I was so
scared that my mind went blank. The horse ran around the log
over and over until Chris' directions slowly began to sink in. It
seemed like an eternity but I finally did it. Chris had me repeat it
a few more times successfully to which everyone clapped and we
were able to move on to the next person. It was all such a blur but
I remember standing there trying to be brave, swallowing over
and over, while the tears welled up. I was just so terrified that I
could not enjoy the success I just had. It was all just so scary. At
that moment I just hated Chris for what he had made me do.
My head was spinning. I wanted to quit and run away. But then
I didn't want to look like a baby and I didn't want to cry. I just
wanted to learn, but I was petrified!

I don't think I realized just how deep my fear went until that
very moment. That was the first time someone had challenged
my fear and didn't let me back down. Prior to that, when I had
expressed fear, my trainers would back off let me off the hook.
Chris knew I was afraid but he also knew that in order for me
to get over it I had to face it and walk through it. It was when I
was challenged to face my fear that I learned what true courage
was! As I mentioned before, courage is being afraid, but doing it
anyway. And the only way one can get over their fear is to face it
head on. This is one of the hardest things I ever had to do. I was

afraid and didn't think I could do it but I did it anyway. This is what you must do too.

Learning About Yourself!

I remember lying awake that night and going over the events of the day in my mind over and over. I didn't want to quit and go home but I didn't want to continue either. The fear was just too great. I kept telling myself I couldn't do it. I worried what the challenges of the next day would bring. Would I be able to do it? So I did what I always do when I can't sleep and I have no answers; I prayed. I prayed to God for strength, courage and perseverance. And then something strange happened that I still can't explain. A feeling of peace came over me along with a sudden realization that I was being defeated by my own self doubt! I sat up and turned on the light and began to write in my journal. I was being negative and sabotaging my own efforts to try and overcome my fears. I needed a new outlook. I needed to be my own cheerleader. If I was going to be successful, I had to be positive!

The next morning, Chris demonstrated to us how to do proper trailer loading. By using the same method as we did the day before with jumping a horse over a log, we were to raise our direction arm and direct the horse's hind quarters into the trailer. After Chris demonstrated this to us a few times he asked who wanted to be first. Instead of positioning myself to the back of the pack and hoping not to be noticed, I raised my hand and said, "I will!" With my new-found positive attitude I confidently marched up to the trailer. Instead of telling myself "I can't do it" like I did the day before, I quietly whispered to myself, "I can do it, I can do it!"

On my first try the horse ran around my direction arm and did not load into the trailer. Chris corrected my arm position and explained that I had actually directed him to the left around me instead of into the trailer. The next try I did it! I raised my direction arm and he walked right into the trailer. I did it again and he went in again. I will never forget the self satisfaction that I felt right then. I had made up my mind to be positive and to face my fear and I did! My new attitude produced the results I was looking for! This is what I want for you. Attitude is everything and having a good one has everything to do with how successful you will be…no matter what you are doing.

With a few more terrifying moments that I will share in the next chapter, I made it through the week with a sense of courage and confidence that I hadn't ever felt before with regards to horses. But this was only the beginning. Chris offered me the opportunity to attend Horsemanship II four weeks later and I jumped at the chance to go back to Texas and learn more. This time there were only three other people there. Three of us had participated in the clinic four weeks prior and one man was new and was a young reining trainer. We started out on the ground again but our tasks were much more demanding than in Horsemanship I.

Since Chief had only been in training with Chris for about four weeks when I had arrived there for Horsemanship I, I didn't work with him much. But during the second clinic Chris had me working on the ground with him. He was young and feisty and tested every ounce of courage I had. I remember it was February and it was drizzling outside. We were all wet and cold. Chris had us lead our horses down to a pond. The banks were muddy and slippery. He had us direct our horses into the pond and then they were to turn face us. They were not allowed to move until we directed them out of the pond. When my turn came, I directed Chief into the pond and he turned and faced me. He became impatient and starting pawing the water, splashing me with muddy water. I was freezing and drenched from head to toe but to my amazement he did not move until I directed him out. When that day was over I took a hot shower and attempted to dry out my boots but the satisfaction of success was greater than any discomfort that I had experienced that day.

The next morning was again brisk and cold. I went to get Chief out of his stall and he was totally full of himself like a bee at the end of a string. He was jumpy and energetic and I worried I wouldn't be able to handle him. He reared up, threw his head, and pranced around me until he was actually running around me as if to lunge. I remember Chris saying earlier, "If they act up or are impatient, give them a job to do," so I started letting him lunge around me. Chris came out of the barn and saw what was going on and yelled out, "Disengage Heidi, disengage!" "What?" I thought. I couldn't remember what I was supposed to do to get this crazy young horse to stop and face me when he was running around me like a wild stallion. I remember yelling back to Chris, "I'm in over my head here!" I think he was disappointed in me since I didn't have a clue as to how to settle this young horse down. But my mind was blank and all I could think of was to stay out of Chief's way and not get hurt. Chris marched over and sternly guided me as to how to disengage Chief's hips so that he would stop, turn, and face me. When it was over I shook like a leaf. The whole experience, with this young horse seemingly out of control really scared me, and set me back again. Again, I began to wonder if I could continue. What had I had gotten myself into by purchasing Chief when not only I didn't know anything, but neither did he?!?!

Determined not to give up, I continued the clinic and finished with a deep sense of accomplishment. I had gained a lot of confidence around horses and had begun to let go of some of my fear. Much to my surprise, I felt that the insights that I had learned about myself as a person far outweighed the horsemanship skills that I had learned. However, this was just the beginning into my journey of understanding and overcoming my fear. And it was certainly just the beginning into my long journey in training Chief which included some of the most harrowing experiences of my life that I will get into in another chapter. But again, I did not give up.

Unfortunately at that time I did not realize that I was really a beginner rider. I had *thought* that I was an intermediate rider. Knowing what I know now though, it is clear to me that I was truly a beginner and had no business buying an untrained baby colt. I would have gotten much more out of the horsemanship clinics if I had more riding experience prior to attending and if I had a more experienced older horse.

Chris Cox teaching Heidi about confidence by having her stand up on the back of a horse.

Another exercise in confidence. Heidi riding bridleless and without reins. No holding onto the saddle horn either.

CHAPTER 6

Green on Green

My Journey With Chief

As I have said over and over; a green rider on a green horse is not a combination that I would recommend to anyone, especially someone with fear issues. My decision to buy an 18-month-old untrained colt was one of the dumbest things I could have ever done. Every chip was stacked against me. But there was something about Chief that I felt deep down inside of me: a kinship, a bond, and I wanted him to be mine. But this decision made for some of the most uncomfortable, emotionally diverse and educational experiences of my life! Rick Lamb told me, "My advice to anyone considering buying a horse is simple: Take your time, be honest about your abilities and situation, and choose a horse that fits you today, not tomorrow. You will grow to love any horse. In short, choose with your brain. Your heart will follow." This is great advice that I wish I had known back then.

From the day I first saw Chief on that brisk fall day I was smitten! He was gorgeous! Another common mistake that novice riders do is buy a horse based on his color! Most horses are beautiful anyway and color should be your last criteria when you are searching for a horse to buy. But, like many others, I was looking for a certain color rather than a good match. My decision to buy him was based on several things:

1. I had been looking for a reining prospect and I was told his father was a champion reining horse.

2. I had always wanted a black and white paint horse.

3. Since I couldn't afford a finished reiner, I looked at the cost of his training as a kind of payment plan.

Here's how it turned out:

1. Chief's sire, Range Cheifton along with his grandsire, Hank A Cheifton, were both world champion roping horses, NOT reiners.

2. You should not buy just for color as "pretty" is not the smartest criteria for buying the right horse.

3. I probably spent over 5 times in training what I would have spent on an already-trained horse.

It is worth mentioning that Chief and my story did not begin easily. A woman I knew casually had actually bought Chief a few weeks after I had first seen him but before I had a chance to get the money together. I was crushed. But his owners were anxious to sell him as they were going to take him to a Paint Horse auction the following week. So with no other choice, I relented and told Kimberley she could buy him.

Another month went by and all I tried to do was find another "Chief". I looked and looked until I found a website that offered several different black and white paints for sale in Alabama. After speaking with the owner and viewing a video of several prospects I chose a two-year-old colt with a background that included Peppy San Badger and Two Eyed Jack in his breeding. Mind you, I never saw this horse in person which I have to say was a huge mistake.

I had them geld him for me and then I arranged for him to be shipped from Alabama to Chris Cox in Texas for training. I was so excited. I could hardly wait to hear what Chris thought of him once my new horse arrived. A few days had passed and then I finally got a call from Chris. He asked me if I knew what I had purchased. I found this question rather odd and asked him to explain what he meant. He said, "This horse is u-necked, cow-hocked, extremely obstinate and only stands about 13 hands tall!" Oh my gosh, what had I done? "What?" I said. He said, "Heidi, you got yourself a camel!"

My heart skipped a beat as my mind began to race. What was I going to do now? After a lot of thought and much discussion with my husband, I called the woman that I bought this horse from. I asked her to recall our conversation where I told her that I was 5' 7" tall and was looking for a horse that would reach at least 15.2 hands. I explained to her that the horse I bought from her would never grow to be that tall and that a horse under 15 hands simply wouldn't work for me. I held my breath as I waited for her response. Her words were music to my ears. She told me that she stood behind all of her horses and that she would gladly refund my money if he was not what I wanted. The following week she arranged for a trailer to pick up the horse and I received a refund check in the mail. Her integrity restored my faith in humanity. It goes to show you that there are honest people in this world.

Once word got around that my "dream horse" purchase did not turn out well and I was again looking for another "Chief", I received a phone call from Kimberley. She told me that she heard what had happened and that she felt deep down that Chief was supposed to be *my* horse. She had only owned him for two months yet she was offering him to me. She said if I didn't want him she would keep him but "if you want him he's yours". I couldn't believe my ears. It was a just few days before the New Year and three days later he was loaded in a trailer on his way to Texas.

Chief did well with Chris Cox. He quickly found out that he was a very sensitive horse who got his feelings hurt easily. Yes, as funny as that sounds, Chief still does not respond to harsh reprimand and he'll only dig in his heels more if he is treated heavy-handed. I found that what works for him is unemotional consistency. You must ask him patiently, yet consistently, and then you reward him with relief (or removing the pressure). So when he does something wrong, I correct him immediately and then ask him firmly yet gently again until he gets it right. And then, boom, it's over. I don't dwell on it or belabor it. But this concept wasn't understood by me right away.

After 5 months in Texas he came home to California and I put him in reining training where he began to excel rapidly. Everyone was excited about his athleticism and talent. He did even better with cows so we started him with some reined cow work. About 6 months into his training we had just brought him back from a work out with cows. He suddenly collapsed in his stall. He wouldn't get up even when the feed truck dropped off his dinner. I called the vet out the right away. He had me send him around in the round pen first at a trot and then at a gallop and then he'd listen to Chief's heart. What he found was that Chief's heart was not beating in a constant rhythm but was erratically racing and then dropping suddenly which was causing him to be exhausted. The vet told me that I needed to take him to the closest equine hospital and have an EKG and some other tests done on him right away.

I was worried sick about my beautiful and talented young horse. At the hospital, it took five days for Chief to learn to how to walk, trot and gallop on a tread mill before they could actually perform the EKG. The doctor at the equine hospital told me he had seen this condition before in young race horses. It is called Exercise Induced Brady Cardia. Sometimes young horses can't handle the stress of training. After all they are just two-year-olds! The doctor compared it to five-year-old children starting kindergarten; some are mature enough and ready to learn and some have to wait another year to start. I was advised to take him out of training and put him out to pasture for 90 days of rest and let him grow up a little. Easier said than done.

In Southern California, finding pasture space near the city is next to impossible. At the time, I was still boarding at a public stable so I was going to have to find a place for Chief to go since there was no pasture boarding available where he currently was. I searched and searched until I found a lay-up facility in the local mountains. It was about a 35 minute drive up winding roads but Chief would be able to take it easy in a huge grassy paddock. It looked like the ideal place that any horse would love.

It was about a month into the stay when I realized how much Chief missed me and how lonely he was there. The other horses were far away in their own huge pastures. They don't combine horses in this facility as they all have "issues" and it would not be wise to subject them to the potential kicks and bites of new pasture-mates. So when I came to visit, Chief would dance the jig when he saw me and then scream in agony while running along the fence next to my car when I would drive away. It broke my heart and yet it amazed me that he was so attached to me. I just couldn't stand seeing him like this so I brought him back to the boarding stable a few weeks early. We started just hand-walking, giving him turn-outs and then slowly brought him back into training.

Sadly, he was not the same talented horse he was before he got sick. He was awkward and off-balance and seemed not to be enjoying his training. He began to balk during his workouts to which the trainer would unsuccessfully try and reprimand him. This turned into a battle of wills to which there were no winners. Both horse and trainer were frustrated. It was about this time that many other mysterious ailments began to pop-up. Chief got mouth ulcers, many saddle bumps (Easophylgranulomas), and a horrible case of chronic diarrhea. He just wasn't thriving and finally got so sick that he spent two weeks in the equine hospital while they ran test after test but could not diagnose his condition. Finally after putting him on orchard hay the diarrhea subsided only to return with a vengeance 10 days after I brought him back to the boarding facility. Besides a bad case of tape worms, yes *tape worms,* they could not find anything medically wrong which would cause all of this. He spent another 3 weeks in the hospital and the doctor finally determined that it must be stress that was causing Chief to be so sick. When I asked the doctor if he was going to be okay she replied wistfully and somewhat doubtfully and said, "I hope so." I was feeling panicked because Chief was just not thriving but no one seemed to know why!

The doctor suggested that I take him out of training, change his environment, and give him lots of rest. Again, easier said than done. Boarding facilities in my area all had long waiting lists. The places I did find that had openings, were far away from where I lived and I felt I needed to be close to Chief to monitor his frag-ile health condition. Then Kimberley (whom I first bought him from) said I could keep him back at her house. She lived about 15 minutes from my home and with only two other horses in her backyard I felt this would be a quiet peaceful environment for which Chief could recuperate. I put him on a special bland diet, got him regular equine massage therapy, chiropractics and many other holistic treatments and supplements. My once strong spir-ited young horse was frail, weak and depressed. I was sick with worry. Many nights I laid awake with worry over him. He was not out of the woods. Everyday that I saw him my heart sank when he seemed to not be improving. I cried and cried. Within about two months I began to see small signs of improvement. He appeared to have gained some weight, his eyes were becoming brighter, and his previous listless demeanor showed signs of playfulness.

A few weeks later a well-known Western Quarter Horse trainer in my area called me to tell me that she had an opening in her barn for training. I was a little worried that it might be too soon for Chief but she was familiar with what I had been through with him and we agreed that she would take Chief very slowly and very gently. Her training sessions started out with easy 15 minute rides. She asked very little of him. She did this for about two months before his sessions slowly increased both in time and demand. She understood his personality and tried to teach me the correct way to school him to keep all parties from getting frustrated. She was very successful in getting Chief back into shape and begin his training again but unfortunately she did little to help me improve on my riding skills. In short, she was great with Chief but not great in teaching me.

It was after about a year with this trainer that my husband and I bought our small ranch and moved our horses to live at home. This proved to be the best place for Chief as physically and mentally he thrived in our no-stress environment. It has been over 9 years since Chief has lived with us in our backyard and I am happy to say that he evolved into the greatest mature horse that I had always hoped he would become. He is well-trained, kind, gentle, reliable and trustworthy. Another once-in-a-lifetime-horse! The close bond that we have formed is one that I always had hoped for.

With his training now finished by Carolyn, along with her expert help in teaching me what I needed to know to become a skilled and fearless rider, I am finally enjoying the level of horse-manship that I always wanted for myself. It was a long journey filled with many ups and downs but it was all worth it in the end. Chief and I are lifetime partners with an unspoken agreement between us that we will always take care of each other. I thought this kind of a relationship was only written about in storybooks. But I am here to say, it is not only a reality for me, it is also possible for you.

Heidi and Chief, sorting steers.

CHAPTER 7

From Fear Into Confidence!

Following My Friends on their Journey

Once my fear melted away and my confidence allowed me to relax and enjoy riding, my need to help others overcome their fear became a priority. Only someone who is plagued with fear, yet loves horses, can understand what an accomplishment overcoming their horse fear really is. I began to talk to many people about their fear level and soon realized that this problem was much more common than I had originally thought. When you are stuck in fear, it is easy to feel like you are alone in fear. Not true. There are many people who are right where you are; frustrated and confused!

Brenda, Jamie and Callie are friends of mine who agreed to allow me to follow them on their journey from their horse fear into confidence. I am so grateful for their willingness to contribute their stories to this book in hopes of helping you through your fear and restoring your confidence after a horrible horse accident. Whereas I had deep-seeded fear of horses from a bad experience in my childhood, I had never been badly hurt from a horse-related accident. It is my hope that their stories will both inspire and encourage you to work hard to get back into the joy of fearless riding.

Brenda and Jamie's Story

This story is unique from the prospective of how a horse accident that happened to one person affected, not only the victim, Brenda, but also her daughter Jamie.

From the time Brenda was 10 years old growing up in Michigan she worked hard to be able to ride horses. She collected bottles to turn in for money to afford to rent a horse on the weekends for $1.25 per hour. By the time she was 15 she and her best friend had saved up their money to buy a horse for $100.00 and they kept it in a garage down the street. Grass hay was 50 cents a bale. They had no money for tack so they rode bareback. She was fearless and would ride any horse at any time with no formal training. She grew up and became a nurse, joined the Air Force, and got married. In her late twenties she started taking English Hunter/ Jumper lessons. She was still young and fearless and fell off many times but it never bothered her. As she got older and was busy raising her children it was always her dream to buy another horse. By the time she was 39 she finally did. A few years later she bought two Arabians that were supposed to be child-safe. As it turned out they were wild and not well-trained but she found a great western trainer that taught the Arabs to cut cows. Imagine that? But Brenda said they were "great". At that point her trainer found her a dead-broke Quarter Horse which turned out to be a wonderful teacher that got her into Quarter Horses and into the Western method of riding. This horse was a great experience for her and she kept him until he died at the age of thirty.

When Brenda's daughter, Jamie, was 12 years old the family moved to a farm in Virginia. That was when Jamie began her true experience with horses. Jamie said that she never really felt like an experienced horseback rider. She distinctly remembered her mother telling her over and over to "be careful you're going to get hurt." These words were always in the back of her mind. So Jamie never really felt like she was fully in control of any horse she rode but when she did ride, she said she remembered that she had fun. Sometimes the horses on her farm represented "work" to her with all the feeding and cleaning they required, so along with school, sports and friends, Jamie found other activities at that time that she enjoyed more. After graduating from high school she went onto college and then, like her mother, she joined the Air Force as an officer. Her job was such that she was one of only four or five women in an environment of all men which required much skill. In other words, Jamie was no wimp! She did three tours of duty in Iraq and one tour in Afghanistan. It was after her first deployment to Iraq that everything changed for her with regards to her relationship with horses.

While Jamie was home on leave, her mother, Brenda, thought it would be fun to saddle up their horses and take a ride with a couple of friends. Brenda was riding her three-year-old filly named Champagne Wishes that was newly broke. Brenda had some concerns about this young horse because she had her with a trainer who she thought had made the mare a little bit sour. On that day she was riding her with a new and very stiff leather saddle. After a little while, Brenda had asked "Wishes" to canter. At that moment, her friend, who was riding another horse, came up behind her so close that they brushed up against Wishes' side. Wishes bucked. The second time around the exact same thing happened again; her friend brushed up against Wishes' side and she bucked again. Only this time it was much harder. The new saddle slipped and Brenda's foot got stuck in the new stiff leather stirrup. She knew that she should try and jump off so she quickly pulled out her other foot and threw it over the saddle horn and managed to pull out her stuck foot out from the stirrup. Just then, Wishes bucked again and shot Brenda up in the air like a rocket. She slammed down hard on her right shoulder when she landed. She tried to get up and that is when she realized that she couldn't move and was hurt very badly. Jamie got off her horse and ran to her mother's side while their friend called 911. She cradled her mother's head in her lap for 1 ½ hours and listened to her agonizing screams until the ambulance came. Once at the hospital, they found out that Brenda had broken her arm in four places. This is when Jamie realized how serious her mother's injuries were and she began to be physically sick with worry about her mother. The next day Brenda underwent surgery and to make matters worse, she almost died because of a pre anesthetic complication. After four days in the hospital she came home and for months could not lie down. She had to sleep in a reclining chair. For another six months she did intensive physical therapy which was, in her words, "agonizing". She developed lymphedema and then breast cancer. She went through radiation and five years of medication. But in all this time she kept her passion for horses and riding. But fear had set in and she developed a paralyzing fear of cantering her horse. You can imagine how witnessing this accident affected Jamie's confidence also. She watched the whole thing as well as watched her mother's agonizing recovery which planted a seed of fear in her mind that would grow into her own personal fear that she would later have to work to overcome.

A few months after the surgery Brenda did get back on Wishes and walked her around here and there but she didn't really ride her seriously for another three years.

Meanwhile, Jamie was on her forth deployment in Afghanistan when she called to talk to her mother. Both remember that it was Mother's Day. At that time, Brenda had been looking into different clinicians and decided that she should attend a week-long clinic called Building Rider Confidence. When Brenda told Jamie of her plan, Jamie decided that she should also take the clinic and work on her confidence also. By now, Jamie was 29 years old and had begun her search to purchase her own horse.

I wish I could say that all went well. But as you know, sometimes well-laid plans don't always turn out the way we hope. A few months before the clinic, Jamie purchased "Jed", a five-year-old

Quarter Horse. She was told he would be a good horse for her so, on the advice of a trainer, she bought him. But what is important to remember is that just because a trainer can ride a horse well, doesn't mean a novice can do the same. Jamie's lack of confidence and Jed's lack of training made for a difficult partnership. Frustration set in and only made matters worse. Jamie's dream of owning her own horse was not going the way she had hoped.

So both mother and daughter set out on a three-day-drive pulling a horse trailer through four states. They arrived at the horse clinic along with Brenda's horse, Bear, a horse that she had purchased to ride while Wishes was in training and Jamie's horse, Jed; thus beginning their first step into overcoming their fear.

Callie's Story

Of all the people I interviewed for this book, Callie amazed me the most! Her courage and tenacity were second to none. She was bucked off and hurt more than any other person I have ever spoken to, yet she did not give up! She kept at it and kept searching for answers. Callie was so honest with me that she even admitted that she knew all along that it wasn't the horse; she *knew* it was her and her lack of knowledge, yet she wasn't going to stop until she found the help she needed.

Callie was another "horse-nut" kid that couldn't get enough of horses when she was growing up. She didn't have horses as a child, but she was "horse crazy" even still. When she was in high school, she began hand walking Thoroughbreds at a race track seven days a week from 4am to 2pm. It was then when she bought her first horse for $200.00. Prince was a Thoroughbred gelding off the track. She boarded him at different places and kept him at different friends' farms and actually kept him until he died last year at the age of 31.

As an adult in her mid-thirties, Callie began to participate in Civil War reenactments on a borrowed horse. Eventually she bought a young horse that didn't know a lot who really didn't have any real true training. Callie admitted that she rushed him along to try and get him ready to do the reenactments and she said that she "missed all the signs" that this young horse was not ready. So one day she was decked out in her Calvary costume with pistols and a saber when her horse "blew up" during a reenactment. He started crow hopping, spinning and rearing until Callie flew off and landed on the hilt of the saber handle which became impaled into her shoulder blade on the left side. The medics examined her, bandaged her up, and determined that her injuries were not life-threatening. So they sent her on her way with an ice pack and a lot of Ibuprofen and she managed to finish out the weekend but this marked the day that her fear set in!

"If I could have him back I would do things totally differently", she said recently, "It was a shame because the horse later got injured and was sent to the wrong trainer who couldn't seem to help his bazaar and explosive behavior." Callie remembered, "I used to try and sit real quiet and real calm" to try and keep him calm. "But that damn-near killed me" so she sold that horse. But that was not the end of Callie's bad experiences, in fact, it was just the beginning.

Not too much later Callie was riding her friend's Morgan and it bolted for the barn, jerked and swerved and she flew off and hit her head on a fence. "I took out a board with my head and arm." She said she wasn't really hurt badly but she was sore and "emotionally injured."

About a year later when Callie was in her early 40's, she bought her own Quarter Horse named Monty as a five-year-old. About 30 days later, Monty started displaying many different behavior problems. He was overly sensitive and anxious. Callie soon found out that she could not even look at him in the eye or "he would wig-out!" He began to buck here and there until his bucks turned into full-blown bronc riding and she was thrown off of him several times. She began riding him with full contact on his mouth, holding the reins real tight, in hopes that that would control him better. Callie knew she wasn't doing something right and she knew it had to be her, but with the frustration that had set in and her lack of knowledge, Callie began to lose hope in Monty.

Callie and her family now live on a beef cattle ranch in Missouri. They have five bulls and have about 100 head of calves. So Callie knew she had to learn to ride because her life included using horses to help run the family calving business. Callie also knew that Monty may not be the horse for her so they just bought a couple of dead-broke ranch horses from a sale that were supposed to be good family horses. One day while out looking for stray calves, the horse she was riding, bolted and bucked and threw Callie off into a creek bed where she split her head open and broke her back. The ambulance came and took her to the hospital where they put staples in her head and fitted her with a brace she had to wear from her groin up to her chest. Ironically, Callie holds a Masters Degree in Physical Therapy and even though she took a week off of work, she still couldn't sit down because her tail bone was so sore. It was after this accident that Callie knew she needed to find help with her riding, but where?

With Monty now off with a trainer, Callie began to look for answers. She found the Building Rider Confidence clinic that Brenda and Jamie were headed to and Callie also signed up to attend it. She was thinking that this was her last hope. It had been one year since she had been on a horse. In fact, she had only gotten medical clearance to ride the week before she arrived at the horse clinic. She was excited about attending the clinic but was also terrified to get back on a horse for the first time. Callie opted to use one of the clinic horses rather than bring one of her own.

The First Step

This is where we all met for the first time: Me, Brenda, Jamie and Callie! After introductions and telling "horror" stories, I had a frank discussion with my three new friends. I asked them if they would be willing to let me follow them for a year, tell their terrifying stories, and document their quest to find their confidence again in hopes of helping other people get through their fear. They all agreed. None of us knew how it would turn out, especially me, but they were willing and I was grateful for the chance they all gave me to be a witness on their personal journeys.

Heidi with her three new friends. (Photo by Crystal Gibson)

It was evident from the beginning that all three women had to forget what they thought they knew about horses and start over. They spent the first couple of days relearning the basics and grasping the importance of proper ground work. This was practiced over and over in many different situations until the correct use of ground work was mastered by all. All this repetition was designed to eventually transfer what they had learned on the ground into the saddle. By the third day it was time to mount their horses as the instructors wanted to evaluate each rider's skill level. So everyone had to walk, trot and canter in a round pen, one at a time. Brenda and Jamie had been on a horse recently but were not comfortable cantering. But for Callie, this was the first time she had been on a horse since her accident. I watched her gather up her courage as she mounted one of the clinic horses, having no idea what to expect from this gelding. Her face was white as a ghost and she told me she felt like she was going to "puke". At one point the instructor had to remind her to breathe. But she did it; she got on the horse, rode him, and even cantered him.

When it was Brenda's turn to canter she said her heart was up in her throat. Bear was a handful for Brenda because he had a fast canter and it felt like he was always going to run off with her. But she did it also. When Jamie began to ride Jed in the round pen, she couldn't get him to stay on the rail. When she asked him to canter he seemed to kind of lose control of himself and throw his head like a young colt on a crisp cold day. Jed's lack of training just added to Jamie's frustration and didn't help her progress much. But all three women did express a great sense of accomplishment at this first step into pushing themselves through their fear. There was more repetition and different exercises during the week and on the last day there was a trail ride. Callie's horse lost his footing and slid down into a creek and Callie had to jump off. But she was such a trooper. She simply got back on and hid any trace of being terrified.

Like I said before, there is no quick-fix. It takes commitment to change which includes time, energy, and, of course, courage. Brenda, Jamie and Callie had begun their journey into fearless riding. The week-long clinic did help build their confidence but their training would have to continue once they got home. When Brenda got home she sent Wishes to a trainer for several months. Soon after, Brenda began taking lessons on her. Within two months she got up enough nerve to ask the mare to canter. She was terrified but she did it; only a couple of strides at a time, but she did it. The trainer made sure that, not only was Brenda ready, but that the horse was also ready. The first time she cantered Wishes around the entire arena, Brenda was thrilled. "It felt good but I was still apprehensive." she said. Even though she felt great about this accomplishment, the fear was not gone, but she had taken a huge step towards overcoming it. After about a year at home, she had decided that it was time to invest into another week-long horsemanship clinic to build on what she had learned the year before.

Jamie and her mother, Brenda, live a few states away from each other and after a frustrating week at the clinic with Jed, Jamie was convinced that he was not the horse for her. So Brenda bought him from her and put him into training. "He is a different horse," said Brenda. "I tried to convince Jamie that she should bring Jed to the second week-long clinic a year later, but Jamie felt more comfortable using a clinic horse for this next week."

Callie felt that she was sent home with a lot more solid knowledge and with the advice to find a horse that she was comfortable with to continue to work on her riding at home. She worked with Monty on ground work when she got home even though he was not making a lot of progress with the trainer to curtail his bucking habit. "Do I keep him or sell him?" Callie wondered. Callie rode another family horse at home and worked on building her confidence and she felt that bringing Monty to the next clinic was the next step in overcoming her fear and continuing on her horsemanship journey.

A Year Later

It had been nearly a year since we had all been together at the first clinic. We had spoken by phone and communicated through email throughout the year but we were excited to meet up again and share in the next step into their journey of confident riding.

It was at the second clinic that Callie was taught to work on raising her energy in order to raise the energy of the horse, rather than try and be quiet and calm in the saddle (because she thought this would keep the horse calm). When you raise your energy and thus the energy of the horse, you are teaching him to think and focus on you as the rider to guide him. When a horse feels the rider take charge, he begins to calm down and respond to the rider's commands. An instructor worked with Monty for only 15 minutes and showed Callie how to yield Monty's hind quarters and get his feet moving. This short period of instruction taught both Monty and Callie what her trainer back home couldn't master in the past year. Callie learned to raise her energy in an environment where it was safe to try it. "Now I feel like I have the knowledge to work with him at home safely and build on what I learned in the past week."

On the fourth day of the clinic, Brenda, Jamie and Callie were all mounted on their horses in a huge open field dotted with trees. The day before, they had ridden and cantered in a large arena and felt pretty good about it thus far. But cantering in an open field without the perceived safety of a railing was still another big challenge. They were first asked to trot around a tree to practice their ability to control their horse's direction. All were successful. Soon they were asked to canter in the open field using all the tools they had been given; yielding the horse's hind quarters, direct reining, proper posture and seat position.

I stood there and watched as Brenda, Jamie and Callie began to canter their horses out in the open. I held my breath because I remembered how terrified I was the first time I did this with Carolyn back at home. But the feeling of exhilaration once you realize you that you are in total control of the horse, and he is not going to run off with you, is indescribable!!! The huge smile on Callie's face, the image of Jamie not wanting to stop cantering, and Brenda's squeal,

"I got my joy back!", was a moment I will never forget! I felt so privileged that I was allowed to be a witness as all three of my friends overcame their fear and gained their confidence right before my eyes! The memory still brings tears to my eyes!

Callie's smile! (Photo by Crystal Gibson)

Jamie cantering! (Photo by Crystal Gibson)

Brenda overjoyed! (Photo by Crystal Gibson)

At the end of the week I asked Callie if she had made the decision about whether she was going to keep Monty. "Yeah, why wouldn't I? He's done everything I have asked of him." She added, "It was my issues, not his." Callie had been given the tools to bring Monty back home to her farm and begin a partnership with him.

What I want to emphasis here is that over and over it was proven to me that it wasn't the horse that was the problem (although many times, novice riders try to learn on a horse that is not suited for them) but it was the rider that was causing more and more frustration to the horse. Once the horse begins to feel frustration, they begin to sour. Every time the fearful rider begins to saddle the horse, the horse feels the anxiety and begins to brace himself for more confusion and frustration.

When Brenda got home with Wishes she kept saying over and over, "She is a different horse!" But what Brenda hadn't realized was that Brenda was a different rider! The combination of a confident rider and a no-longer-confused horse made for a great partnership! Brenda now knows that she has a new mind set.

She had to throw away all the old prior horse knowledge that she had and start over and rebuild herself, not just as a horseback rider, but as a horsewoman!!!

Jamie has been very busy at her job in the armed forces since she got home from the clinic. Brenda took Jamie's horse Jed home and put him in training. Brenda said that Jed is a different horse also. Once Jamie is ready, she will bring Jed home and begin building her partnership too. But the few times Jamie has been able to ride since the clinic, she has felt a lot more confident and feels like she has the tools to handle the horses she has ridden.

All three women have successfully overcome their fear and begun to enjoy their horses again! As Callie told me recently, it is a "process". Everyday that she goes out to ride, she has a plan in mind. She is focused and works to improve on her riding all the time. It took a lot of courage for these three women to get their confidence back but none would give up. This unbelievable tenacity is how you define 'passion'! All three women's passion for horses was bigger than their fear!!! All three continue to be eager to learn more!

CHAPTER 8

The Women Speak!

Insight From Stacy Westfall and Karen Scholl

Stacy Westfall is currently one of the most successful female horse women in the country. I would venture to say that you have probably seen her world-famous You Tube video of her dressed all in white, mounted on a beautiful black horse, riding in a freestyle reining pattern completely bridleless and without a saddle. The first time I saw it, I was moved to tears because I realized what kind of expert riding skills it would take to do something like that. But more importantly, I was struck by the emotional connection between horse and rider in order to be able to communicate with a horse on that kind of level. Imagine how much trust and understanding both horse and rider must have mastered with one another?

When I first saw Stacy's video I had no idea who she was, but I was determined to find out. I began to follow her career and read several articles she had written or that were written about her. I soon found out that she had recently won the colt starting competition at the famous Road to the Horse in the Spring of 2006. Then she appeared on the Ellen DeGeneres television show because even Ellen wanted to meet the woman in the famous video that had been viewed over a million times.

You might think a woman like this was such a good and accomplished rider that she would never have any kind of fear issues with regards to horses. This would be the logical assumption, but you would be wrong. Every single person alive has had to deal with some kind of fear on some level at some point in their life and Stacy was no exception.

Back in 2004 Stacy had just started a two-year-old filly named "Maggie" who was a "quirkie" mare, for lack of a better term. She was not a typical filly who fit into the usual training timeline mold and Stacy knew this. Maggie was requiring a lot more time and a lot more repetition than the average colt that Stacy was accustomed to training. One day Stacy went out to the barn to work with Maggie. Normally when Stacy is working with a horse she is very in tune to her emotions.

"I know my emotions," Stacy told me. "One thing that makes me a very successful rider is being able to know what my emotions are when I am working with a horse."

"I can only be in tune with my horses if I am in tune with my own emotions," she added. Now think about this statement for a minute. What is your emotional state when you are working with your horse? This is a very important aspect of successful horsemanship yet frequently ignored by most people and on this day, this is exactly what happened to Stacy.

As Stacy approached the barn to work with Maggie on this day she knew she was working against a time line. Stacy had discussed with Maggie's owner that she was taking longer than most colts with her training. But even with this fact being understood by all, Stacy was still feeling pressure on this day. Her mind was filled with deadlines, commitments, sick kids, household duties and horses that needed training. It was during this time that many opportunities were presenting themselves to Stacy and she wanted to pursue them all!

Stacy told me over and over with much emphasis that deep down she knew the filly was not ready to move forward in her training on that day, but she ignored her intuition and pushed onward even though she knew she was not in the right frame of mind to be working with a young horse on that particular day.

"It wasn't that I skipped any of the steps but I just wasn't doing them well" Stacy admitted. "So I got on, got off, got on and got off and attempted to get Maggie ready for her first real ride with me on her back." Everything seemed fine until Maggie started to take a few steps and then got scared. Stacy felt her tense up and before she knew it, Maggie had jerked the reins through Stacy's hands and bucked hard. "I knew she was the type of horse to lose her mind and 'go blind' when she exploded."

"Things were not going smooth even before I ever mounted", she said, "I wasn't thinking about her emotions or my emotions," As the mare's explosion built and she bucked again all Stacy thought about was getting off so she swung her leg over and jumped off. "She wasn't ready and I knew it!"

The mare went one way and Stacy went the other way and the mare stopped and looked at Stacy no doubt wondering what was coming next. After both horse and rider had calmed down, Stacy went back several steps and picked up the ground work again teaching the filly over and over, day after day, to where she got back on successfully and Maggie ended up being just fine. Stacy was reminded that all horses are different and don't always fit into the same mold whether it is training or their emotions. They have different personalities and need to be dealt with individually. "Maggie woke up in me the fact that I needed to be more aware!"

"I was so mad at myself for ignoring my feelings and therefore ignoring the steps", she said, "I really had to think about it, get it out and figure out what went wrong so that I wouldn't take it into the barn again". Then Stacy realized, "It was an opportunity for me to learn more about myself".

Have you ever really thought about your horse fear as an opportunity to learn more about yourself? Again, use your journal and really think about your emotions. Learn from what Stacy had happen to her as an example of what you can wake up in yourself. Understand that we all make mistakes and luckily our horse friends are very forgiving. But the key is learning from your mistakes and therefore correcting them.

Childlike Ignorance Can Be Such Bliss!

You know when we are kids, we don't really have much fear. Ignorance is such bliss at this stage of our lives. Stacy told me that when she was six years old she fell off her pony and broke her arm. She lamented how she could remember that it hurt as well as many other details of that incident but she does not remember having any fear about it. "There are pictures of me on the pony a few days later with a broken arm!"

But Stacy remembers very well the day she first became aware that there is a certain amount of inherent risk involved with riding horses. "It was the first day that I mounted a horse after I had just had my first son." It wasn't that I felt fear, it was that I felt aware that someone else was depending on me and that I didn't want to get hurt". Before that, she doesn't ever remember having any thoughts about fear at all.

I can relate that to when I first went skiing again after taking several years off when I was raising my three boys. When they were all old enough, my husband and I took them up to the local mountains to teach them to ski. We put them in ski school and we headed off to the slopes to do some skiing on our own. I know it had been a few years but I was really having a hard time getting comfortable skiing again. I noticed that I didn't want to go as fast and that I was leaning back in my boots. I remember my husband asking me what was wrong to which I replied, "I don't know, I feel like I've lost my nerve."

This was the awareness that Stacy was talking about that I, too, began to feel for the first time. That vulnerability that I was not young and reckless anymore and that I didn't want to get hurt because I had three kids to take care of. This is the very same emotion that takes place with many of us with horseback riding also. Even with an expert like Stacy Westfall!

I spoke to so many people, men and women, about this "awareness" that hits us at one time or another. It is usually associated with some sort of close-call as we mature where we realize we don't want to get hurt and so we back off with our reckless abandonment that pushed us to the extremes we felt when we were younger.

Stacy successfully trained many colts over the years in between training Maggie and starting Maggie's first foal. "Even though we had bred her to a stallion that we hoped would mellow out her baby, which it did perfectly, I still compared this colt to his mother." Stacy felt the fear again the first time she mounted Maggie's colt. "So I did the same thing with him that I did with his mother to get over the fear. I repeated the training steps over and over until I was back into awareness but had not crossed over into fear."

Awareness vs. Fear

Let me repeat this: 'Into awareness but not into fear'. Think about this statement. These are very insightful words and worth emphasizing. According to Merriam-Webster, Fear is defined as: to be afraid of, expect the worst with alarm, apprehension, safety of one's life. The definition of awareness is: watchful, having or showing realization, perception or knowledge. Wow! What a great lesson from Stacy. To sum things up, she worked with the colt on the ground over and over until her apprehension of expecting the worst turned into her being watchful and having realization, perception and knowledge! This is what you need to do too. Get back to the basics of groundwork with your horse and practice over and over until you no longer feel apprehensive yet you are still watchful. I will talk about going back to basics in more detail in Chapter 9. Right now, let's get back to Stacy and her experience with helping people with their fear issues.

Stacy has dealt with many different people with fear issues and as a result she feels that there are different degrees of fear. And like I said in Chapter 1, Stacy agrees that you cannot begin to work on your fear until you identify it. Some people are not aware of their fear which, Stacy has found, makes it harder to fix. "They might have enough fear to be tense but not enough fear to identify it," she said.

This is why self awareness is so important. On the other hand, Stacy said, "not having enough fear to know you need more knowledge can be a problem too." You must be able to admit that *you don't know what you don't know.* Back in Chapter 5 when I spoke of my ground work experience when I was trying to direct a horse over a log and have him turn and face me, I remember that was the moment that I realized how much I didn't know about horses. Up until that point, I still thought I was an intermediate rider! Stacy feels that it is very important to only do what you are comfortable with until you are ready to move on. "Know yourself," she said, "Know where the line is that you are at and work towards crossing that line."

"Get off if you are worried," she said, "I tell people all the time; do what you are comfortable with and then put your horse away and go and analyze it." Here again is an opportunity to write in your horse journal. Self analysis is not a simple process. It takes hard work and dedication. "Your fear is telling you that you are feeling a lack of confidence and a lack of confidence is due to a lack of knowledge," Stacy added, "Find the knowledge before you force yourself to cross your line of comfort!"

Stacy Westfall

Karen Scholl

Teaching professionally since 1995, well-known equine behaviorist and clinician, Karen Scholl, offers her program "Horsemanship For Women" throughout the United States and Canada. But don't be fooled by the name since just as many men attend her clinics as women. By respecting the diverse learning styles of both genders, Karen recognized that men learned by 'doing' while women needed time to 'process' the information.

We all know that it is common knowledge that most men won't read the directions or ask for directions, they just plunge in and 'do it'. But women are emotional, many times to a point of avoidance. They think about something, then they have to think about it some more, then dissect it to think about it in a whole new way, and then they call their friends to talk about it even more. Right? I know, because I am a woman. When Karen saw these different tendencies between men and women she used them as an opportunity to design her clinics in such a way that the information could be totally understood by everyone.

Karen's experience with her clinic participants proved that, "Every person I encounter is experiencing some degree of emotion, whether it's fear, uncertainty, curiosity, frustration, excitement... or some combination thereof! People process new experiences similar to horses, which is to feel uncomfortable when faced with anything new, different, sudden or abrupt. And just like horses, when the person recognizes that the person guiding them has their best interest at heart, is more than willing to give them the time to 'get it', and appreciates their efforts to try, everyone relaxes and finds they can actually *enjoy* their learning experience!"

So a variety of different people come to Karen's clinics and most of them experience some level of anxiety. "We tend to put a negative emotion to our problems," she said, "and often times trying new things takes us out of our comfort zone and that's where 'good-enough' comes from." Karen feels that where our horsemanship is concerned we should use every problem as an opportunity to learn more and then "never stop learning and think we know enough...ever!" Instead, we want to continually evolve from:

- *Unconscious Incompetence* into

- *Conscience Incompetence* and learn the skills to go to

- *Conscience Competence* and if you keep learning, you'll go into

- *Unconscious Competence!*

So how do you start this ever-evolving journey into competent horsemanship?

First of all, Karen believes that it takes "a high level of curiosity and humility". Add to that: Time, commitment and willingness to stick-to-it! She agrees with every other expert that I talked to that starting on the ground, with proper and repetitious ground work, is where we all need to begin.

Karen told me that at the prestigious Spanish Riding School in Vienna, students work on the ground with horses for two years before they ever get on a horse's back! Once they finally mount a horse, they still don't use reins or stirrups. The instructor uses a longe line or stands behind the horse using long draw reins while the student works on proper balance, independent seat position and proper leg position! This intense training continues for another two years before the student begins to ride solo under the watchful eye of the instructor.

Karen explains, when after only two or three days at her clinic her students sometimes ask when they are going to get to mount their horses, "You *are* riding your horse," she tells them. "You are learning to ride on the ground. The lead rope is your reins." So everything you learn on the ground you will learn to transfer onto the back of the horse! "I break down the *purpose* of ground work," Karen said. "I simplify things and teach my students that they are training their hands to communicate with their horse through feel!" Karen's students begin to use *feel* to move the horse's feet, the hip and the shoulder.

Remember when I told you how uncomfortable I was with the ground work that Chris Cox was trying to teach me? This is an indication of how poor of a rider I was at that time due to my lack of understanding of proper horsemanship. Practice is where physiology kicks in after repeating ground work exercises over and over. "Anything new is going to feel awkward," Karen said, "It takes practice to build the muscle memory that it takes for something to become familiar." Just like when you first learned to swim or tried to snap your fingers for the first time. It felt different, awkward, maybe even a little bit scary until enough practice turned it into something you didn't have to think about anymore. Well proper horsemanship is no exception. The definition of communication with the horse is being understood by him!

Karen's personal goal with horses "is to be able to go anywhere at any time, do anything I want to, and have fun doing it!" She asks her students to ponder this statement and rather than be frustrated with themselves or their horses, try to thinking, 'I may not be good at the activity, but my horse and I will be having fun taking our foundation of communication into new and different situations!'

This personal goal is in contrast to the more common scenario of what Karen calls the "conditional relationship" that many people have with their horses. They'll ride in the arena, but not out in the open; or alone and not with a group; or with a group and never alone; and never on a windy day! "That was me, at my early stage of horse ownership, and mostly because of what others around me were doing or saying to do," Karen said, "I find now that when horses feel they have a real leader and 'job' to do they are quite trusting and adaptable."

Do any of these "rules" sound familiar? Because a conditional relationship with your horse is an indication of fear and "fear is an indication that you are not prepared," Karen said, "Your gut is telling you that you don't have the proper skill set to be able to respond, not if, but when something were to happen." So we tend to set up *rules* to try and limit and avoid any possible situation that could reveal we are not prepared. Instead of doing that, we need to use our intellect to seek out professional coaching to sharpen our horsemanship skills. And learning to become comfortable with anything new and different helps people build the confidence to try more new things and encourages them to continue to learn to further their skills of effective communication with their horses.

Karen Scholl

CHAPTER 9

Let's Hear It From the Boys!

Sound Advice From Richard Winters, Steve Halfpenny and Mike Kevil

The one thing that I heard over and over, from every expert that I spoke to, was that when you are experiencing fear, you must take several steps back; back to basics! Once you have had an incident that has shaken your confidence, it is essential for you to go back to where you are comfortable and then build from there. I can't emphasis this enough.

I remember many years ago, I began golf lessons so that I could play the game with my husband. Actually, my golf pro said that I was "a natural" and apparently I had a pretty decent swing. For months and months I took lessons and practiced until I could hit the ball pretty straight and pretty far. One day, I started to shank the golf ball over and over until I was so frustrated that I could barely hit it at all. I remember the golf pro saying, "shorten up your swing". He had me only use a half swing until I got my swing back in control. This is also the same concept that is useful for building your confidence with horses.

Steve Halfpenny

Australian horseman, Steve Halfpenny, first became a Pat Parelli instructor in 1995. But his constant search to better understand horses and improve on his methods was further inspired by such greats as Ken Faulkner, Phillip Nye, Buck Brannaman, and Ray Hunt. His goal was to get inside of the head of every horse he encountered and help educate horse owners about the importance of this concept. "I teach leadership, not dominance," he said.

When Steve begins to help someone with fear issues, he first asks you to analyze your fear. Then he has you take yourself back to the place where you *are* comfortable. If you are okay brushing a horse, then he starts there. At the point where he might ask you to saddle your horse, many people might begin to get nervous to where Steve asks them 'Why are you nervous?' "They assume that if I'm asking them to saddle up, I'm going to make them ride," he said. The same concept goes for cantering. Many people fear cantering their horse. "So I ask them to trot, and only trot, until they are trotting fast enough that the horse may break into a canter, to which I say, 'no, stay in a trot'. At the end of the lesson, I ask them, 'Did you realize that you cantered four times today?' But if I had told them they were going to canter that day, they would have been scared," he said. "As soon as they think they might 'have to' then the emotions come up," he added.

Steve feels that horses mirror the people who ride them. If you are scared, then your horse is going to be scared and that is how the vicious cycle begins: You get on a horse, get scared and stiff, the horse feels it and gets upset and the result is another bad horse and rider experience. This will happen over and over until you make a decision: Either you stop riding or you stop being afraid.

"Sometimes someone tells me that they are afraid and I get on their horse and I don't feel comfortable on him either," Steve said. Many, many times people have a reason to be afraid because their horse is not right for them. Actually, it is a common problem for people to have a horse that is not a good match for them which only intensifies the issue of fear.

Steve Halfpenny

Richard Winters

Horseman, Richard Winters, couldn't agree more! "Sometimes you've just got to cut your losses," he said. "As an instructor, I first analyze the situation. I assess the level of the person's fear and the horse that they have. Sometimes there is nothing wrong with the rider or the horse, but together, the two are not a good match."

Richard Winters did not grow up on a farm or in a horse environment. But it was always his dream to become a cowboy. His parents were not horse people, so you can imagine their response when all Richard wanted to do was be around horses. During the summers of his teenage years he worked at summer camp wrangling dude horses. He then worked for the accomplished horse trainer, Troy Henry, and later enrolled in a farrier program, until he eventually wound up in one of the best rodeo college programs in the country. Through the years his horse handling skills became more and more refined as his career as a horse clinician evolved and flourished. In 2009, Richard became the coveted winner of the famous Road to the Horse Competition.

Richard knows what it does to his own confidence if he gets bucked off a horse. "I'm only half the rider that I was when I get back on, and I'm a professional, so I can only imagine the anxiety felt by the average person," he said. So he asks his student to analyze what happened before the bad experience happened. Most of the time, people have a pretty good idea what went wrong but just as often, people don't understand the reason the incident occurred, "Horses don't just do things for no reason!" he said. Sometimes we are oblivious to the reason because of our own lack of knowledge.

Richard feels that many times we confuse our horses with mixed signals. We are out of balance and hanging on too tight to the reins. We ask the horse to walk and then we pull back on the reins and everyday we are just sneaking by "like walking across a volcano on a bridge with rotten boards," he said. "We think, 'Whew, I didn't get hurt yesterday, I hope I don't get hurt today'!" This is no way to be and this is why it is so important to learn to ride properly.

Another common horse fear issue is that people are afraid to canter their horses. "I would be afraid *not* to canter my horse," Richard said. "Everyday you don't canter you just make it worse which makes it a bigger problem in your mind." Richard teaches his students the importance of an independent seat in the saddle. "Too often I see people using the reins to hold on but we all must learn to ride balanced and independently," he said. Relying on the reins creates a very dangerous sense of false security in the mind of the inexperienced rider. "But it's like anything you want to learn to do well; you have to put in the time," he added.

Richard explained to me that we don't put our kids in school and then only take them there when we have the time. We commit to making sure that our kids go to school everyday. Learning proper horsemanship takes the same commitment. "Nothing is natural," Richard said. "It is learned; the same goes for horsemanship." We must remember that "horses are not natural leaders; they are natural followers." Richard emphasized that if we ride as if we are the passenger in the saddle instead of the driver, we are frustrating our horses since they look to the rider to guide them. And remember that a frustrated horse becomes a sour horse. This is why it is so important to learn to become the leader if you are going to be successful with your horse.

Richard feels that it is the rider's job to help their horse become brave. So how do you teach a horse to become braver? "Capitalize on the horse's curiosity," Richard said. There are many exercises you can do to teach this. "Let them follow what they are afraid of," he said, "a bike, a cow, a tractor or whatever." Slowly you will see a horses fear turn into curiosity and slowly he will begin to settle down and get comfortable.

To build confidence, Richard suggests giving the horse and rider a job! "You can't think about fear and the job at the same time," he said. The same goes for your horse! All of the experts that I talked to all agreed that setting up a game on horseback or giving your horse a job to do is a great tool for building confidence and helping to put your fear out of your mind. I can relate to this even now when I take Chief cow sorting. Before we get into the pen and start sorting out the cattle I can feel Chief's anxiety which naturally makes me tune in to it. But once they say "go" we both forget about the anxiety and just go to work!

Richard Winters

Mike Kevil

Mike Kevil wrote the book on colt starting. Literally. As the author of the book, "Starting Colts" and four-time Road to the Horse judge and one-time "surprise" competitor of the competition, Mike Kevil, has been dealing with the fear of horses and the fear of people all of his life! He feels that horses and people parallel each other where fear is concerned. "Their fear is the same," he said. "What is different is that people lie and horses don't!" Mike knows that as soon as he begins to work with a horse the horse is going to show him his fear and reveal what he doesn't know. But a person won't usually be so forthcoming. They will usually try to hide their fear and try to gloss over what they don't know. "But that's okay, it eventually comes out," he said. "I treat training people and training horses the same. I desensitize to remove the fear, then work on getting more control, and then build the trust which leads to more confidence." It sounds so simple yet so worth repeating:

1. Desensitize

2. Achieve Control

3. Build Trust/Confidence

Mike desensitizes in small amounts because it is easier for both the horse and the rider to advance a little at a time. Then if fear sets in, he takes them back to their comfort zone which is just a small step away. Once they are comfortable, he begins to build on it again. Mike told me that he only asks for a *try* because you need to have a balance between pushing too hard (which can lead to trouble) and not pushing enough (which gets you nowhere). "There is nothing wrong with stopping when discomfort sets it, but there is something wrong with not trying," he said.

Mike explained to me that fear of the unknown is defined by worrying about something that *might* harm you. This is a result of lack of experience and lack of education about any given situation. However, if someone gets hurt on a horse, this becomes *known* fear and therefore avoidance sets in. It is logical to want to avoid something that you *know* might harm you. "But either fear, known or unknown, I treat it the same way," he said. "The more education and skill you have the more you can be assured of the outcome."

Mike likes to always finish a training session (either with a person and /or a horse) on a good note. This positive sense of accomplish sets up the next training session to be something to look forward to rather than something to dread. Sometimes if a trainer pushes you too fast and too hard, you may think to yourself, 'thank God it's over', but are you going to want to do it over again the next time? This is why balance in training is so important. "You can't wish away fear," Mike said, "it's going to take work." The work should not be traumatic, but it should be consistent and methodical!

Mike Kevil

CHAPTER 10

Practical Secrets to Success

This final chapter will attempt to explain various different practical concepts that you can work on when you are beginning the journey to overcome your fear. Let's look at what we have learned so far. All of the experts that I talked to about horse fear unanimously agreed that in order for you to overcome your fear you must first start by doing the following:

1. Admit your fear.

2. Define your fear.

3. Start at the point where you are comfortable and build from there.

Then seek out professional advice to learn:

1. If your horse has had enough training and then decide whether together you are a good match.

2. Learn proper ground work and practice over and over before mounting up.

3. Transfer your ground work to the back of the horse and begin to learn proper riding in the saddle.

Continue:

1. As you go back to the basics you must take the time to practice over and over until your correct horsemanship skills becomes second-nature.

2. Every time you saddle up you must tune into your emotions and formulate a plan for the day's session.

3. Get your mind off of your fear by playing games on horseback or by giving your horse a job.

What Worked For Me!

The following are more hints that really helped me that hopefully will help you with your horsemanship.

<u>Your</u> Body Language

"Don't be pensive!" These three little words were one of the most important hints that I was ever told and have never forgotten. It was said to me by a one-armed cowboy I knew who was delivering my horses to me once we had moved to our new ranch. I was leading one of the horses in front of him and my body language revealed to him exactly what I was feeling. If he could see it, then the horse could feel it! Right? The horse had just gotten off the trailer and was in a new and strange place so naturally he was nervous and jumpy. This made me nervous and jumpy. Remember horses are looking to us for reassurance so if we don't give it to them then they are not going to calm down. I have replayed those three words in my head over and over when I have needed the reminder. I realized that I had to be confident in my body language even if I didn't feel confident inside. You don't slink up to a horse. You walk up to them with purpose and authority using strong, erect and assertive body posture. You must be in control. You are what your horse is looking towards to overcome his natural fears.

Leading Your Horse...The Importance of Yielding The Hind Quarters

When leading your horse you must relax both of your arms down by your sides. Your hand should be no closer than six to eight inches from the clip on his halter and the lead rope should be loose with slack. Try not to choke-up on your horse's lead rope and grip under his chin with your arms stiffened. This tells the horse you are not relaxed so therefore he will not be relaxed either. This goes back to what I said earlier, that you must own up to your part as to what you are doing that is actually keeping your horse from being calm. Walking nervously and stiffly with your horse will never get him to relax. It has to come from you first.

If you think you can control your horse by holding his head tight you are headed for problems. There is no way you can control a 1000 lb. horse by his head. It requires the skill of controlling his hips. One of the things that Chris Cox drilled into my head over and over was the importance of knowing how to disengage your horse's hips. If you are going to control a horse it must be done with his hind quarters not his head. This is basic ground work that should be taught to everyone before they ever get into the saddle. As I have stated over and over, proper ground work is the foundation for proper riding.

I heard the well-known horseman, Jon Ensign, say that the secret to horsemanship is teaching a horse where to put his feet. "If you can control his feet, you can control his mind," he said. Simply put, yet so important to remember!

While there are no short-cuts to becoming a fearless rider, there are secrets that will help you get to where you want to be. The following are more practical hints that helped me. Once I applied to them to my riding, I started to see measurable results.

In the Saddle

Since I ride Western I can only tell you what worked for me from a Western point of view. When you are in the saddle there are a few things that you must master if you are going to be successful. Some of these exercises might feel strange at first but work on one thing at a time in order to make these techniques become second nature to you. These hints really helped me and I still use them as part of my mental check list to be certain that I am not getting lazy.

Assuming that you know how to properly saddle your horse, start at the beginning with proper posture and continue working on each exercise until you are comfortable enough to build on it and move on to the next step:

1. **Proper Posture** - I really had a hard time figuring out where my proper posture in the saddle was supposed to be. So I used this simple guideline until I could do it without thinking about it. Sit up straight and suck your stomach in. You will feel your bottom tuck under as a result. Now relax your leg muscles by the horse's side and try and keep

that as your correct posture position. Practice this at the walk until it begins to feel more natural. Once you have mastered the feel of your posture you are ready to move on to your proper feet placement.

2. **Heels Down** – If your heels are not down, it means that your toes are pointed downward and that will naturally make your body want to pitch forward. When I first started to concentrate on keeping my heels down it felt really awkward. I had to really practice this a lot both in the arena and out on the trail. To learn this, try the following exercise: Once the balls of your feet are secure in the stirrups, drop your heels. Now relax your legs and your knees. Do not try and brace yourself by straightening your knees and putting pressure on your feet in the stirrups. This will cause your legs to extend out to the side and make your knees very sore. Simply drop your heels and relax your legs gently next to the horse's sides. Keep this as your feet and leg position. There is never a reason to slide your entire foot into the stirrups, point your toes downward, or stiffen your knees. You want relaxed leg contact with your horse's sides. Learn how to give leg cues without lifting your heels (this was really hard for me to master). Practice this over and over until the position becomes second nature to you. If you are still unsure try this exercise: Take your feet out of the stirrups and drop your legs down to the horse's sides. Note how your legs look; relax them yet keep your heels down. Now repeat the first exercise again by putting the balls of your feet in the stirrups and dropping your heels. Try and mimic your foot and leg position while your feet were not in the stirrups. Also, take note if your stirrups are either too long or too short and adjust them accordingly. Note: Your stirrups

should be shorter than when your legs are hanging out of the stirrups. If you are still unsure about your stirrup length, have a professional help you. Remember, stirrups are just a place to rest your feet.

3. **Don't Lean Forward** – This was probably one of my worst habits and the hardest for me to break. Leaning forward naturally tells your horse that you want him to move forward. By keeping your correct posture and your heels down it will naturally help you keep from leaning forward. Hunker your bottom down into the saddle and relax your hands and shoulders. Practice your posture and keeping your heels down while trotting and loping your horse. It is easy to do this at the walk so work on keeping your butt in the saddle while the horse is in a faster forward motion

4. **Don't Hold the Horn** – Every time I thought the horse was going too fast or that I didn't have control, I would grab for the saddle horn. This gives you a false sense of security. You must learn to ride *with* the rhythm of the horse. Holding onto the saddle horn fights your motion against the movement of the horse and makes your body stiff which makes you ripe for falling off. Relax and go with your horse's movement.

5. **Give Your Horse His Head** – I used to think that if I held my reins tight with both hands and had constant contact with my horse's mouth I would be more in control. Not only is this not true, it is another example of having a false sense of security. All you are really doing is contributing to your horse developing a hard mouth and communicating to him that you are tense. Relax your hands and ride with draped reins. One of the scariest exercises I ever

did was to practice loping my horse one-handed with a draped rein. My teacher made me do this over and over. It was very scary because I thought I had no control but then I actually realized that I did have control with my legs. Learn to ride holding your reins with one hand if you can. I now ride with a lot of slack and by holding the reins in my left hand. Use your legs to ask your horse to go left or right rather than your reins. If you need to switch to two hands or choke up on the reins you can slide your free hand up the reins for closer contact. Practice switching from one hand to two hands over and over so you can switch over without having to think about it.

6. **Breathe** – Take deep breaths and concentrate on your surroundings (rather than what you think your horse might be thinking). Don't look at his head or look at the ground when you are riding. Look where you are going (or at the scenery) and try and focus on the beauty of the trails rather than worry about your horse. Trail riding has become so therapeutic for me that my mind is like mush by the time I get home.

7. **Relax** – When you are tense, the horse can feel it and in turn can become tense also. This means that neither horse nor rider is enjoying the ride. Read all of the riding hints I have listed above again. Count how many times I use the word 'relax'. This is the key to fearless riding. Just relax. It helps to meditate on this especially before you ride. I pray before I ride. I pray for safety and I ask God for protection for myself, my friends and our horses.

8. **Stay Calm** - There is one rule of thumb that you must never forget: *Always stay calmer than your horse,* even when you

are facing danger. Never lose your cool and more importantly, never lose your temper with him! You can be firm and assertive but always be in control of your emotions. Patience is the key to success! Dr. Robert M. Miller told me that if you are experiencing any of the following emotions you should not be working with your horse: Anger, Frustration, Impatience or Fear. Horses are very keen at reading humans. This is why overcoming your fear is one of the greatest things you could do for your horse!

Try Singing

I have to laugh when I talk about this one hint as I figured it out quite by accident. For ten years I sang in my church choir. As a result, I was constantly going around singing hymns. When I started to feel nervous, either on the ground or in the saddle, I would hum or sing. I found that this not only helped to distract my fear and settle me down, it also had a calming effect on my horse! Singing is good for the soul and I believe it is also good for a horse's soul. So sing away your fear, it really does help.

Who is Spooked: You or the Horse?

Probably one of the hardest aspects to get over, when you're trying to overcome your fear, is the constant nagging in your brain that your horse could spook at any given moment! It becomes a sort-of "preoccupation" with most inexperienced riders. Believe me, this worry is very much sensed by your horse thus making the likelihood of them spooking much greater. I used to ride with a group of ladies who constantly pointed out what they thought could be potential dangers to each other. "There's a tractor up on the left", "there's a plastic bag in that bush over there", or "there's a rabbit in the brush". While this might seem like a polite gesture of caution, it also causes your brain to be in a constant state of uneasiness for what potentially might happen in your mind. We cannot be a fearless rider if we are constantly looking for danger. Being cautious is one thing but being overly cautious is defeating the purpose and is contributing to the problem. We must relax and 'go with the flow' so to speak. Other than being very frightened on the ground with a horse, the thought of my horse spooking was terrifying. I simply didn't know what to do if he did.

A good rule of thumb to remember is that if you are calm, your horse will stay calm. Good words, but how do you stay calm? One thing I learned that really helped me was to stop always looking at my horse's head. Every time my horse would perk his ears I was scouting the area for the potential "spook". This does not make for a relaxed rider. Instead, this is an over-cautious rider who is not helping keep his horse calm. But how does a fearful rider stay calm and stop looking for danger? Some call it desensitizing or "sacking out". Chris Cox simply chooses to call it *preparation*. Just the thought of this concept terrified me. Why would anyone want to try and intentionally spook a horse with a fearful rider on his back? Let me repeat once again, that if you are ever going to overcome your fear you must face it head on. Of all of the exercises that I have ever done, this was by far the scariest but, at the same time, it was the most useful tool in helping me overcome my fear of my horse spooking. Fortunately for me, I didn't know it was coming so therefore I couldn't obsess about how scary this exercise was going to be prior to it happening. Let me explain.

On or about the fourth or fifth day of the first Chris Cox Horsemanship Clinic we were all mounted on horseback in a large arena. We had just finished an exercise and were waiting to hear what we were going to do next when Chris walked purposefully up to me and the horse I was on, suddenly took off his hat and began waving it wildly in front of my horse's face. The horse naturally spooked and immediately tried to turn and run off. I was so shocked and angry at Chris for doing this to me, but before I could say anything in protest, he began to give me verbal instructions as to what I was to do to keep the horse under control while he was being spooked. He kept on walking towards the horse and continued to scare us both and continued to explain to me what to do to control the horse. "Direct rein" he said. I was to keep the horse facing the fearful situation and not let him turn away. Once he was satisfied with my attempt, he proceeded to do the same thing to the next mounted rider and the next until we had all experienced what many of us feared the most. But what we had done was face the fear and learn what to do in the situation instead of just fearing it or hoping it wouldn't ever happen to us.

When a horse spooks, his natural "flight" instinct tells him he should turn and run from the potential danger. Your job as the rider is to keep him from doing just that. Keep his body and his head looking at what is scaring him. Use your legs and your reins to make him face it until he settles down. Do not grab the saddle horn! Doing this makes your body fight against the rhythm of the natural movement of the horse. Once you go against the movement of your horse rather than flowing with his motion, is when you can lose your balance and fall off. It is a good exercise to try and keep your body loose like a boneless chicken and learn to go with the rhythm of the horse.

Have a trainer or a friend help you with this as well. It will help desensitize both you and your horse to potential spooks. Once your horse knows you are in control during a stressful condition, he will begin to trust you to take care of him. This is how you begin to build a true relationship with your horse. I know it sounds scary but if you are to get over being worried about your horse spooking, and you want to build trust with him, you must practice this exercise until you are no longer preoccupied with the notion of "what if he spooks".

There was a time when I was in my most fearful place that if a horse spooked and scared me enough, I would never have ridden him again. Even though I remember feeling this way, I can hardly believe now that was once really me! Amazingly enough, the thought of spooking does not scare me anymore. Occasionally I still jump when the horse jumps but more out of being startled than being scared. One of the first things I taught my husband was how to handle a horse when it spooked. Both of our horses tend to want to turn and bolt when they are spooked. But both of us know this and are prepared for it. But the key is that we don't worry about it. Keeping your hips relaxed is very important and will keep your body in rhythm with the movement of your horse and will help you stay with the motion of your horse if he should suddenly spin or turn if he becomes startled.

Remember that your pensiveness, your tension and your uneasiness is never hidden from your horse. It is silently screaming to him loud and clear. Horses are very intuitive creatures that sense everything around them to a much larger degree than most people realize. A horse looks to his rider for confidence and will do anything for a rider that he trusts. How can he trust you to guide him if you are scared to death? That is why you owe it to your horse to learn to overcome your fear, to KICK your fear by facing it and walking through it.

Proper Planning

One thing is clear; riding a horse can be risky. We assume that risk every time we mount up. Riding on trail is even more risky than riding in an arena. We simply have less control over the environment and the little hazards that can pop up without warning. That is why it is imperative to have the proper knowledge and understanding before you saddle up and venture out.

Just like taming a lion is risky, the trainer knows the risk and is prepared. Would you attempt to tame a lion without the proper knowledge? Then why would you attempt to get on the back of a horse without the proper knowledge? Horseback riding takes practice, tangible skills and courage. Let's face it, you're getting on the back on a 1000 lb. animal and giving him control over your safety. So the more you know, the safer you will be. Fear will hold you back and keep you from progressing. Challenging your fear will bring you through it.

Proper planning avoids poor performance! We have heard this statement over and over in our lifetime. It also applies to horsemanship!

Balance

Horseback riding is all about balance, timing and feel. These are the basic components of knowledge necessary for you to be successful. If you can keep in mind these three concepts while you are working on your fear, it will keep your goals in focus.

Have you ever given someone a piggy-back ride and had them not be centered in the middle of your back? You have a hard time walking straight with this heavy load on your back that is not balanced evenly. So now maybe you can imagine what a horse feels when his rider is not centered on his back. Balance is essential for successful riding. It is related to your posture which is why sitting correctly is so important. If you are not balanced you make your horse feel uneasy. Once he is feeling uneasy he can often become annoyed and begin to act up.

I have a friend whose husband is a novice and only rides once or twice a year. Like many novice men, he relies on his masculine strength to ride rather than on any tangible horse-back riding skills. When his horse begins to trot he immediately loses his balance, stiffens his legs out to the side bracing himself in the stirrups, and begins to lurch from one side to the other trying to compensate for his unbalance. It looks as though he is going to fall off any minute. Imaging how uneasy this must make the horse feel. This is where one needs to strive to have a *good seat.* I'm sure you've heard that term; a good seat. It means that you have good balance and your butt is glued to the saddle.

My husband was blessed with a naturally good seat. From the moment I first began to teach him to ride he had good balance and a good seat. He doesn't realize how lucky he is because teaching balance to someone can be very hard to do. Due to my past ballet training, I thankfully have good balance and a good seat. It makes it easier to stay with the motion of the horse even when they spook and turn quickly, which leads us to timing.

Timing

Timing is essential for successful riding as one must learn to reward and reprimand within the confines of proper timing. Rewarding a "try" ten minutes later is not going to teach your horse to understand your meaning. The same goes for repri-manding his bad behavior. I think it was John Lyons who said that you have 3 seconds to respond to your horse's behavior.

I've seen many people let their horse's bad behavior build up until their frustration takes over and they finally lose their temper. Once you lose your temper with your horse you have taken ten steps back from building a bond with your horse. Patience is essential to success. Don't let problems build. Handle them immediately. Reward him when he does something well. Like

Chris Cox says over and over, "make the right things easy and the wrong things hard." Timing is everything.

Feel

Feel is much harder to teach but repetition and awareness make this concept a reality. Having a feel for your horse's temperament, his gait, or his body balance is very important but takes time to master. I have met people who don't have a clue whether their horse is sensitive or stoic. I happen to have one of each.

Chief is very sensitive. He feels everything deep down inside. Chris Cox first told me this early in his training. Being a novice, I didn't fully understand what this meant. But it is clear to me now that Chief is very needy. Cody, on the other hand, is stoic. He doesn't show emotion, pain or even affection. In fact when he does, I feel really close to him as I feel I have broken through his self-made "wall". We as horse owners need to actively seek out what our horse is feeling, we must seek out his personality, his insecurities, and his "issues". This is how we begin to understand our horse's needs and begin to understand what they are trying to communicate to us.

Another aspect of feel is being able to pick up on any hitch in your horse's gait. This is so important to being able to detect lameness. Horse's bodies are very large and very heavy in proportion to the size of their skinny little legs and feet that must hold them up. This is why lameness in horses is such a prominent issue. Detecting any lameness early can head off any potential problems before they escalate into chronic problems. Your horse's soundness is essential for your longevity with him in the saddle.

Cody is only 10 years old but he has a chronic inflammation in his front left heel. In the past he has had to wear special shoes and have it injected occasionally with cortisone (now he is barefoot and healing naturally). But through feel, I am able to detect when it is starting to bother him again. I can feel him drop his shoulder at the trot. Remember that Cody is my stoic one. He will continue to cart around a rider even when he is in pain. It is very subtle when I feel that he is off but the point is that I have learned to feel it.

With Chief, it is obvious when something is off with him. He is very animated and will throw his head and act up until I figure out what is wrong. If he turned up lame he would probably have a pronounced limp to let me know how he was feeling. Many times Chief needs to be reminded to keep his body square between my legs, especially at the lope. I can feel when his body is not square. I can feel when his shoulders are crooked or he has thrown out his hip and I now know how to fix it. But you can't fix what you can't feel.

I am still working on being able to feel when my horses are collected properly and are using their back legs up underneath themselves to propel forward rather than reaching with their front legs. I understand that eventually I will be able to feel them pushing their back up into the saddle. This is considered proper collection.

Ride Many Different Horses

Another way to begin to *feel* is to ride many different horses. I think that every horse has a different feel. This will help you to build your confidence. Once you see that you are in the skill position to handle lots of different horses you will gain a sense of accomplishment and confidence like you've never felt before. Make sure that your riding ability is skilled enough to try this and make sure that the horses you ride are fairly well-trained. Novice riders should not try to ride novice horses (or problem horses) as it will not boost your confidence but simply add to your fear. Whereas riding many different horses that have had a lot of experience with many different riders that possess various levels of skill will create the success you are looking for.

Boarding vs. Horses at Home

I know it is not always possible to have your horses live at home with you. But if you can arrange it, it will be well worth it. I have boarded my horses both in public facilities and at private ranches and while that was the only option for me at the time, there is nothing like caring for your own horses at your own home. Being more hands-on has made me a better horsewoman and has created a much closer bond between me and my horses. Can you imagine owning a dog and having to board him in a kennel where someone else feeds him and you only occasionally go and visit? You wouldn't have the same bond with him as you would if he lived at your house. The same goes for your horses. If you don't have a choice and you have to board, you need to make sure you are physically available for your horse as much as possible, everyday in fact.

Have Fun!

While I never said this would be easy, I did say it would be worth it! I still say that overcoming my fear of horses was one of the greatest accomplishments of my life. I used to imagine what it would be like to ride without fear and just have fun! I am here to tell you that it is better than I imagined. And when I think of how far I have come, I am still really proud of myself because I am doing things that I thought might never be possible. I trailer my horse to lots of wonderful different terrains to ride and I canter out in the open while on trail. I have ridden on the beach, amongst the waves and even swam while on horseback! Chief and I have chased cows and participated in team sorting and cattle drives. We have gone on weekend horse camping trips. We have now begun to train for the volunteer Sheriff's Mounted Posse which requires extensive desensitizing training.

Heidi and Chief riding at the beach!

Once you KICK your fear of horses you too will begin to have fun. Once the fear begins to subside and you begin to trust your horse and your own ability, you will begin to experience the joy of horseback riding like never before. I hope that my experience and these hints that worked for me will begin to help you accomplish this. Remember:

Keep at it. Don't give up. It takes tenacity and practice.

Invest in a well-trained horse and the proper equipment.

Courage is needed to gain confidence and will help you walk through your fear.

Knowledge is necessary to gain the skills necessary to let go of your fear.

Practice, practice, practice! There are no quick fixes or short cuts. The more time you are in the saddle the better you will become. Don't keep reverting back to old bad habits. Force yourself to work on that which feels different, awkward or uncomfortable until it is second nature to you. I guarantee that once you master the correct horsemanship skills all of those feelings will subside. Most people are creatures of habit and old habits die hard. Start over, go back to the basics, set up your own training schedule and work on one thing at a time. Once you gain the knowledge you need, your fear will melt away, and all of your hard work will be worth it in the end.

Patience, patience, patience! This is a process for both you and your horse. It is not going to happen overnight. Mount up, take the reins and begin your own training program. Keep a journal and jot down your plan for yourself as well as your progress. Be realistic and honest. Find a good trainer to teach you proper ground work and proper riding skills. Be brave and push through your fear issues. Then just relax, work on your horsemanship as much as you can, don't skip the necessary steps and try to use some of the tips that have worked for me. Don't let fear rob you of some of the things that life has to offer. The time has come for you to start enjoying your horse. It is time for you to put your fear aside and start having fun. Go experience the joy of a relationship with some of the most beautiful creatures that God ever put on this earth. They were put here for us to enjoy them. They were put here to feed our souls. They were put here for us to love!

Good luck on your journey! Relax and enjoy the ride!

Author's Note

After the completion of this book, an incident happened to me that made it necessary for me to apply my own techniques, once again, to myself. It was so relevant, that I decided that I would add it here as a teaching tool. Here is what happened:

You may remember in Chapter 3, I talked about my husband's horse, Cody, which I referred to as "The Cadillac". After seven years of ownership, and at the young age of 14, we had to put him down in the fall of 2011 after he was diagnosed with Equine Corona Virus for which there is no known cure and no vaccine to prevent it. To make it worse, we were told it was contagious to other horses, so we had to wait two agonizing weeks for the test to come back from Washington State University to reveal whether or not Chief was infected also. By the Grace of God, Chief was cleared.

If you have ever had to put down a horse, or any pet, you know how hard it is. We were so devastated! After about a month of mourning, I started my quest for a new horse for my husband. I looked high and low and went far and wide looking for the perfect horse for us. I rode many, many different horses that were not anything like what they were advertising. A couple of horses that proved to have suitable training turned out not to be sound and did not pass my veterinarian's standards.

Finally, I found a Palomino Paint Horse in McKinney, Texas that was for sale. He sounded perfect! He was 10 years old, 15.3 hands, 1200 pounds, and sound! He was also advertised as "bombproof". Now I am savvy enough not to believe that there is such a thing as a bombproof horse, but seeing those words in print, I must admit, gave me a sense of confidence about what I was buying.

I arranged for "Texas" to be trailered to California and when he arrived, he was totally traumatized. He was so stocked up that his sheath was swollen and made him look like a stallion (if you know what I mean). I had to reassure myself that I had indeed purchased a gelding. He evidently had sweat so much in the trailer that he developed a skin fungus. He began to lose his hair by the hunks revealing horrible oozing bald spots all over his body. He needed to gain weight but I couldn't interest him in food of any kind. He was head shy and didn't want to be touched. He was so withdrawn and depressed that I was worried sick over him. My vet called him "a fixer-upper" and told me to give him a lot of rest, a lot of food, some medication and, above all, a considerable amount of time to recover. He explained that some horses won't pee in the trailer and to compound matters, they don't drink enough water, so their kidneys back up and they start to retain fluids.

After about a month, Tex seemed to be getting better so I decided to ride him for the first time in our arena. He seemed calm, responsive, yet a little rusty on his cues. "No big deal," I thought to myself. "He just needed a refresher course." About a week later, I rode him on the trail for the first time and he did great. He went through water, stepped over logs, climbed hills, cantered through the sand and was very sure-footed. I was very pleased, yet I did notice he didn't really neck rein or respond to leg pressure. Again, it was no big deal. This is something that can be taught easily.

The second time I rode him on the trail, I had hauled him to a winery in Temecula. I helped my husband get mounted on Chief and then went to mount Tex. I put my foot in the stirrup and threw my leg over his back and before I could put my other foot in the right stirrup and get myself seated, Tex surged forward to which I instinctively pulled back on the reins. He instantly started bucking, bronc-style, and sent me flying backwards where I slammed onto the road. I landed on my left hip and just lay there, for what my husband said, seemed like forever. But I was so shocked and in so much pain, I just couldn't move.

Tex had run off which, naturally, made Chief upset. I kept telling my husband that I was okay but to just wait until Chief's feet stopped moving before he tried to dismount. A winery worker brought Tex back to the trailer while horrified wine-tasters called the paramedics. I finally got up with the help of my husband and walked over to Tex. He was nervous and breathing hard as if he anticipated a hard reprimand. I patted him and talked calmly to him and then, before I knew how hurt I really was, I prepared to mount him again.

Even though I was in shock, I *knew* I had to get back on. About that time, the paramedics had arrived and I convinced them that I was okay. I rode Tex around for about 20 minutes until I was in so much pain that I had to get off. My husband helped me hobble over to the truck. He loaded the horses and motioned for me to get into the truck but, I told him, I couldn't move. For three days I could not walk. The 10" bruise that I had on my hip was in full color. My whole body ached from the trauma of the fall. But thankfully, I did not break anything and just had a lot of soft tissue damage.

A month went by before I could even *think* about getting on a horse. I thought a lot about what had happened and kept replaying the incident over and over in my brain. What had happened? I summoned advice from all of my expert friends. I talked to Stacy

Westfall, Mike Kevil and Karen Scholl before Richard Winters invited me to bring Tex to him for an evaluation. Richard only lives about 4 hours north of me, so I jumped at the chance. About a week later, I was in Ojai, California riding Tex for Richard and expressing some of my concerns. I wasn't scared, I was apprehensive. I understood what Stacy Westfall meant when she said she had become "aware".

When Richard mounted Tex and began to ride him around, I saw the horse's wide eye go soft as Richard continued to ask more and more of him. "This horse needs a strong leader!" He exclaimed. Finally, he took Tex through an obstacle course and he passed with flying colors. For the finale, Richard asked Tex, over and over, to put his two front hooves up on a wooden box. He got rewarded for every try by releasing the pressure and allowing him to rest. "He's going to be fine," he said. "You two just need a little time to build some trust."

Heidi watching Richard Winters and Tex. A horse will do just about anything for a rider that he trusts!

On the four-hour ride home I called my trusty trainer, Carolyn Trammell. I told her all that had happened and summoned her expertise to help me with Tex. She worked with him for about two weeks before declaring him to be "a keeper." She reminded me what I had written in this book. "Remember what you tell people?" She said. "Go back to basics!" She was right. I went back to the place where I was comfortable with Tex and built from there.

It has been about 6 months since Tex first arrived and I can say that I am glad that I didn't give up on him too soon. I had forgotten what it felt like to work with a horse to slowly gain his trust. He has truly endeared himself to me with the bond we have worked hard to develop. The more time I spend on his back the more I trust him. I still don't know what happened that day at the winery that caused him to buck me off and I probably never will. But it was a reminder that I always need to be aware, I should never take shortcuts, and that even though Tex threw me off, it proved that I could get back on and ride him again with confidence and joy!

In Memory of
"The Cadillac"

Heidi's husband, Pete, with their late horse, Cody. Rest in Peace!

Made in the USA
Lexington, KY
31 December 2012